PEACEMAKING IN A NUCLEAR AGE

A report of a Working Party of
the Board for Social Responsibility
of the General Synod of
the Church of England

Richard Harries

CHURCH HOUSE PUBLISHING
Church House, Great Smith Street, London SW1P 3NZ

ISBN 0 7151 6573 9

Published for the General Synod Board for Social Responsibility by Church House Publishing.

© *The Central Board of Finance of the Church of England 1988*
This publication may not be reproduced either in whole or in part whether for sale or otherwise by any method without written permission which should be sought from the Copyright Administrator, Church House Publishing, Church House, Great Smith St, London SW1P 3NZ.

Printed in England by The Ludo Press Ltd, London SW18 3DG

Contents

Preface

Colin Thubron, in his travels in the remoter parts of the Soviet Union, describes an encounter with a farmer in the Caucasus.

> 'England . . . England . . .' he mused, ransacking his memory for any fact or image. 'Ah yes! Churchill! . . . I've seen your Queen, Mrs Churchill, on our television. She had white hair and was very beautiful, but her head was sticking out of a tank.' I dimly recognised Mrs Thatcher. This photograph of her visiting a tank regiment had been circulated by the Soviet news media to corroborate her belligerence. 'I don't approve,' said the farmer circumspectly, 'of women driving.'

Alas, not all such misconceptions are so amusing. Misconceptions can lead to war. One of the elements in this report is an examination of the differences in perspective between East and West. These have their roots in history and ideology, as well as the more immediate events since the Second World War. We do not believe that understanding the outlook of another is enough, by itself. As two Italian Princes of the Renaissance agreed 'We understand one another perfectly. We both want Italy.' Nevertheless, it is our conviction that the effort to understand, the attempt to enter into the outlook, with all its hopes and fears, of antagonists, can banish misconceptions and might even bring about the kind of changes needed to build trust.

In this respect our concern has been, in the widest sense, political rather than military. We are agreed that massive arms reductions are possible. But we see this as reflecting a change in the political relationships between the two countries. History suggests that although there is no guaranteed smooth path to a normalisation of relationships real enmities can fade. Mercia and Wessex are no longer at war. Although Sweden and Norway still have a demilitarised zone as a result of the treaty they made not to go to war with one another in 1905 who today would think of Sweden and Norway attacking each other? France and Britain have been enemies in some most vicious wars. But we do not feel threatened today by the French *Force de Frappe*. Reducing dependence on armaments is a Christian imperative. But this is only one element in changing the relationships between states so that they do not feel impelled to threaten one another.

If there is one general conclusion to be drawn from our work, it is the need for Christians to use the opportunity provided by *détente*, the relaxation of tensions between East and West, to make every effort to try to overcome the East-West conflict, to work towards *reconciliation* between East and West. In our view, this involves further reductions in armaments on both sides but, above all, it means a dialogue between Government, Churches, and ordinary citizens in both halves of Europe. This dialogue has to encompass many different opinions and many different kinds of people.

As our concern has been with the political rather than the military, so it has been with Theology rather than Ethics. The General Synod Debate on *The Church and the Bomb* in February 1983 discussed the morality of nuclear deterrence and affirmed by a majority of three to one that it was the duty of the Government to retain adequate forces, both nuclear and non-nuclear, to deter potential aggressors. This judgement is not shared by all the members of the Working Party; nevertheless, we have sought to go on from there, rather than debate nuclear deterrence again. We have tried in the chapters on peace, hope, and the State to offer a substantial theological framework which will help guide Christians not simply on the present issue but on other forms of conflict in the years ahead.

The Working Party reflects diverse views on the issues and this has been valuable. One of our members is not a Christian but has been happy to share in this task because of the seriousness and importance of its subject matter. No less important has been the variety of expertise that has been brought to the task, historical, diplomatic, strategic, military, economic, theological and ethical. The process of working has been as important to us as the result, and offers, we believe, a model for the Church as a whole and for a broader process of dialogue. Each draft has been successively modified by the comments of members of the group so that, despite our different starting points, a real degree of unity has been achieved. The report is not such that every member of the group would go to the stake for every judgement within it but its main thrust is a matter of urgency to us all.

RICHARD OXON

Chairman of the Working Party

Members of the Working Party

Ms Joanna James, Lecturer/Researcher, Centre for Defence and Security Analysis, University of Lancaster. Project Officer Scottish Episcopal Church Peace Project. NATO Research Fellow.

General Sir Hugh Beach, Director of the Council for Arms Control.

Ms Mary Kaldor, Senior Fellow, Science Policy Research Unit, University of Sussex, UK Author of *The Disintegrating West* and *The Baroque Arsenal*.

Professor the Rev. Keith Ward, Professor of the History and Philosophy of Religion, King's College, University of London. Former member of the Board for Social Responsibility.

Mr Alan Brooke Turner, formerly British Ambassador to Finland and Minister at the British Embassy in Moscow. Director of the Great Britain/East Europe Centre.

The Rt Rev. Richard Harries, Bishop of Oxford (Chairman of the Working Party).

Professor Sir Michael Howard, Regius Professor of Modern History, University of Oxford. Vice-President of Council on Christian Approaches to Defence and Disarmament.

The Rev. Canon Professor Rowan Williams, Professor of Divinity, University of Oxford.

The Rev. Prebendary John Gladwin, Secretary to the Board for Social Responsibility (Secretary to the Working Party).

Mr Jonathan Alford, Deputy Director of the International Institute for Strategic Studies, was an original member of the Working Party but sadly died in the early stages of our work.

1
The Christian Concept of Peace

> Peace is the object of all the yearnings of mankind, religious and secular; a vision and a promise, a concept at once mystical and practical, supernatural and political. The very name of that concept—*Peace, Pax, Shalom*—tolls like a bell throughout Western theology and literature. Even the toughest agnostic is touched unexpectedly by those phrases in the Christian liturgy which play on all our profoundest longings; '*the peace of God which passeth all understanding* . . .'; 'My peace I give unto you . . .' and by the vision, which has so tragically haunted Judaic and Judaic-inspired civilisations, of Salem, Jerusalem, the vision of peace. Concepts like this are not to be pinned down and labelled like entomological specimens by international lawyers or political scientists.
> (Michael Howard)[1]

The concept of peace is not to be pinned down and labelled, so that passage warns us. Nevertheless, clarity demands that some attempt be made to define the main senses in which the word peace has been used. Some of the acrimony in the debate about peace in recent years has been due to the simple (or wilful) confusion of different kinds of peace. Peace is a word that carries the longing of humankind. It is also a word that is used to describe a precise state of affairs, namely the absence of overt violence. Confusion is compounded by a lack of suitable terminology. Swedish distinguishes between *Frid*, peace of heart and *Fred*, the absence of war between nations. Welsh too makes a similar distinction between *Tangnefedd*, inner peace and *Heddwch* the absence of violence. In English the same word, peace, is used to describe different phenomena. Three main types of peace need to be distinguished and related to one another.

SHALOM: the Peace in which Everything Flourishes

This is a peace which envelops the whole of human life. It is not just the peace of solitary individuals but the peace of the whole community. It is not only an inward state but an outward condition. It embraces life in its totality, inward and outward; personal, social, political, economic and environmental. The root meaning of the word Shalom means 'whole' and it indicates well-being in its fullness, spiritual harmony and physical health; material prosperity untouched by violence or misfortune. Two particular aspects of Shalom can be noted. First, Shalom includes all that we mean by justice. In this life peace and justice often seem to be in tension. Sometimes we are offered the choice of striving for one or the other and it is not possible to have both at once. Again, in this life, different understandings of justice are often in conflict. But where there is Shalom, all that is indicated by true justice is present.

So it can be said that where God's justice is present, Shalom will also be present. Secondly, the realisation of Shalom, in its fullness, belongs to the realm of hope. Throughout the Hebrew scriptures there is a yearning for the time of Shalom, expressed in unforgettable images. This Shalom embraces the whole created order.

> The wolf shall dwell with the lamb,
> and the leopard shall lie down with the kid,
> and the calf and the lion and the fatling together,
> and a little child shall lead them.
> The cow and bear shall feed;
> their young shall lie down together;
> and the lion shall eat straw like the ox.
> The suckling child shall play over the hole of the asp,
> and the weaned child shall put his hand on the adder's den.
> They shall not hurt or destroy in all my holy mountain;
> for the earth shall be full of the knowledge of the Lord
> as the waters cover the sea.
>
> (Isaiah 11.6–9. See also Isaiah 65.25.)

> He shall judge between many peoples,
> and shall decide for strong nations afar off;
> and they shall beat their swords into ploughshares,
> and their spears into pruning hooks,
> nation shall not lift up sword against nation,
> neither shall they learn war any more;
> but shall sit every man under his vine and under his fig tree,
> and none shall make them afraid,
> for the mouth of the Lord of hosts has spoken.
>
> (Micah 4.3–4. See also Isaiah 2.4.)

In the Hebrew scriptures, as the two quotations suggest, this peace is sometimes envisaged as the abolition of war and the rule over the nations by Israel's messianic king and sometimes as a paradisal existence in which all forms of strife will have been removed. But both sets of images assume that Shalom in its fullness belongs to the eschaton, the final age, when God's just rule will transform and suffuse all things. Shalom is a longed-for peace. Can we hope for its appearance on earth? Or is it a peace that lies beyond the spatio-temporal order? Is it a peace that can be achieved in history or does its realisation lie beyond history? These are questions that will be addressed in Chapter 2 on the subject of hope. Shalom is that state of affairs when God will be all in all, towards which the created order is being led; a vision which one day (within time or beyond time or both beyond and within) will be a reality.

PAX: When War is Absent but Coercion may be Implicit or Latent

Shalom is such a heady notion it is easy for theologians to overlook the vital need for Pax. Any country that has known war on its own soil, or which has been beset by civil strife, knows the great blessing of a simple cessation of hostilities. There is, writes Michael Howard, a bedrock meaning of peace, the simple absence of violence.

> especially random and endemic violence, from the society in which we live; the absence of armies traversing and re-traversing the land, burning, raping, plundering, killing, whether those armies are official or unofficial, organised and uniformed or mere robber bands; whether they inflict destruction with knives or from a safe distance with bombs. Peace is the simple assurance that one can sow a crop, with some hope of reaping it, build a house with good hope of living in it, raise a family, learn and pursue a vocation, lead a life which will not be interrupted by the incursion of violence, by physical destruction, wounding, maiming, torture, deaths.[2]

It is not to be thought that the people of Israel, in their longing for Shalom, were insensible of the benefits of Pax. On the contrary, on many occasions we read the phrase 'and there was peace between Israel and . . .'. This is contrasted with another state signalled by a no less frequent phrase 'And there was war between Israel and . . .'. Shalom of course includes amongst its benefits the absence of violence and sometimes, in their longing for a kinder future, it was security from the threat of harm that was to the fore:

> Thus says the Lord of hosts: Old men and old women shall again sit in the streets of Jerusalem, each with staff in hand for very age. And the streets of the city shall be full of boys and girls playing safely in its streets.
>
> (Zechariah 8.4–5)

It is difficult to find an adequate one line definition of Pax because a state of affairs where war is absent can also be one where coercion, in one form or another, is present. This coercion may be basic to keeping war at bay, as in a system of mutual deterrence, or its impact may be minimal. There is no war going on between the USA and the USSR but coercion, in the form of mutual deterrence, is fundamental to their present relationship, and, many would argue, to the absence of war. There is no war going on between the USA and Canada and the coercion implicit in their relationship is less obvious. But it is not totally absent, for Canadians are conscious of pressures of various kinds from their more powerful brother.

The extent to which one believes that coercion, in one form or another, is present in all relationships between organised groups, will affect the definition of Pax. If it is judged that coercion is always a factor then Pax will be defined as armed peace.[3] The problem with defining Pax simply as an absence of war or absence of violence, is that it ignores the many forms of implicit coercion. The *Pax Romana* did not feel much like peace to the Donatists in North Africa, or the *Pax Britannica* like peace to Zulus in South Africa. Indians in North America, Maoris in New Zealand, and Aborigines in Australia are at peace with their white populations. But few today would argue that it is a peace free of coercive elements. We read of Solomon that

> he had peace on all sides round about him. And Judah and Israel dwelt in safety, from Dan even to Beer-sheba, every man under his vine and under his fig tree, all the days of Solomon.
>
> (1 Kings 4.24–25)

A highly desirable state of affairs has been described. But the verse begins 'for he had dominion over all the region west of the Euphrates'. The next verse adds that 'Solomon also had forty thousands stalls of horses for his chariots and twelve thousand horsemen'.

The peace under Solomon, which later generations of Israelites tended to idealise and for whose restoration they prayed, was a peace based on dominion, a peace dependent on suppressing the opposition in the surrounding lands, a peace based on the strength of vast numbers of horses, chariots and horsemen.

Even when military might is not as blatant as it was under Solomon there are forms of coercion no less painful to those who suffer from it, forms of economic coercion that are virtual slavery. Sometimes those who speak vehemently for peace as an absence of war can be blind to hidden forms of economic coercion in society. It is difficult to find a definition of Pax which does not assume either that all Pax is coercive or that no coercion is present. The definition chosen here *Pax: when war is absent* but *coercion may be implicit or latent* does not seek to prejudge any issue, simply to reflect the fact that a state of 'absence of war' may be one in which goodwill and economic co-operation are basic to the relationship and coercion is minimal or one in which war is kept at bay only by the mutual fear of the consequences of going to war.

Societies are held together by a mixture of coercion and consent. Neither, by itself, provides a strong enough adhesive. If income tax was purely voluntary who would pay it? The minimal essential conditions for any kind of properly human life depend in part on the ability of the government to enforce its policies, whether or not everyone entirely agrees with them. This means, in specific terms, the presence of a police force, courts of law and the army. There can be no human community and therefore no properly human life without a measure of just and peaceable order. This is established partly by ensuring that, consent or no, it is not in the interest of individuals, or groups, or nations, to break the peace, disrupt the order or violate the norms of justice. Thus Pax has as its prime concern the absence of overt violence so that individuals can plan their lives on a predictable basis and pursue their goals unhindered. The overt violence that has to be kept at bay is not simply that of the criminal elements within a population but the hired killers of oppressive dictatorships and the unprovoked aggression of invading forces.

It is tempting to make a total distinction between the legally authorised forcible restraint necessary to hold a society together, and the kind of violence that may be unleashed by war. But the distinction is not absolute. The destruction caused by war may be horrifyingly greater than the legitimate pressure used by a state for internal control. Nevertheless, no state can create an oasis of peace in a world of unbridled anarchy. Its internal peace and order depends, in part, on the maintenance of a wider environment of peace and order. The power of 'non-violent' strategies is sometimes appealed to. In certain contexts they can be highly effective, as Gandhi found in India and Martin Luther King in the USA. But 'non-violence' is often used for tactics which are in fact a mixture of pure persuasion and coercion by indirect means, e.g. strikes or boycotts.

Pax does not itself bring about that flourishing of the whole community which is defined as Shalom. It seeks to create and maintain the conditions without which there can be no opportunity for flourishing. Its purpose is similar to the 'Pax' which children call to one another after they have been fighting together. For one reason or another the children agree that they have had enough; it may be that they want to engage in some more enjoyable activity or it may be they are getting too hurt. Whatever the reason, in the interest of both parties, they agree to a cessation of rough and tumble.

Coercion, overt or implicit, is a permanent feature of sinful human existence. Individuals, groups and nations have an ineluctable tendency to pursue their own interests without taking the interests of others into account. Worse still, they can deliberately negate the interests of others. Sometimes this ruthless pursuit of self-interest at the expense of fellow creatures is clothed in moral rhetoric, political ideology or religious demagoguery. This is not simply a re-emergence of an animal instinct for survival. It is also a failure to come to terms with a desire to place ourselves at the centre not only of our own existence but that of others as well. Self-interest and the will to survive, which within limits are proper in themselves, become transmuted into the desire to dominate. It is for this reason that morality and religion can make matters worse as well as better. They can be abused to reinforce a sense of rightness and superiority over others leading, at worst, to a crusade mentality when the enemy are seen as God's enemy. True religion, by contrast, is rooted in repentance, not simply at an individual level, but at a cultural, racial and national level, leading to an awareness that even when there is 'just cause' there is frailty and sin on both sides. Armed conflict is not only due to differences of perspective, or even to differences of interest. There is also at root the desire to dominate or the will to survive. History can be read, with Marx, as a history of economic domination in certain forms. Economic power is not the only form of power, however, and financial thraldom is not the only form that domination takes. The tendency to dominate can be clothed in moral, religious or ideological rhetoric. True religion has much to say about this, both in exposing it and in leading us to repent.

Nevertheless, although true religion has this role it does not always exercise it; sometimes, as history reveals all too clearly, it makes matters worse. So religion considered as a human phenomenon cannot be relied on to keep the peace. If there is rampageous power it must be kept in bounds by checks and balances. In the world in which we live, a world in which power relationships have not been abolished, power must be balanced by power, lest one becomes a tyrant over other states: though this will not prevent it being a tyranny in its own borders. In a world where self-interest has not been transcended and where the self is always liable to become over-weening, organised interest groups have to be tamed by keeping before them the consequences of the unbridled pursuit of their aims. Pax at its highest, where the element of consent is large, partakes of Shalom. Where the element of consent is small, the role of coercion will be large. But whether large or small we need Pax, for without a just and peaceable order no other human enterprise is possible.

Inner Peace

The longing for an inner peace or serenity, what Wordsworth

called a 'Central peace, subsisting at the heart of endless agitation'[4] is widespread. It has also been disparaged as a luxury of the bourgeois class, the expression of an inner discontent that can be afforded only by those with an outer content in more than their fair share of this world's goods. From a Christian perspective this is only a portion of the truth. For the Christian faith offers an inner peace which is not to be accounted for wholly in sociological or psychological terms. It offers an inner peace that is a personal participation in Shalom; a fragmentary anticipation, by a particular individual, of that Divine peace which one day will embrace the whole of existence. Shalom may be, in its fullness, a transcendent vision. But at one point at least it can always be apprehended: by the individuals in their own personal lives, in whatever circumstances they find themselves.

This peace is, in essence, a fruit of the union of the human will with the divine will. For the Christian this union has been achieved, for all people of all times, by Jesus Christ. Our peace is a sharing in that unbreakable union he has eternally with the Father. In Christ there is a union of God and humanity, of earth and heaven, which can never be broken. Through faith and baptism Christians share in this union. So the Christ of the Fourth Gospel told his disciples:

> Peace I leave with you; peace I give to you; not as the world gives do I give to you. Let not your hearts be troubled, neither let them be afraid.
>
> (John 14.27)

So it is that when the risen Christ in John's Gospel greets his disciples he says 'Peace be with you'. This was the standard greeting at the time but its repetition in the resurrection stories in John 20 are a clear echo of the peace of Christ promised earlier. This is a peace integrally linked to the death and resurrection of Christ. Because he has descended into hell and been raised again there is indestructible union of God with people, through Christ, even for those in the midst of hell.

Paul makes the same point in his letters. He writes to Christians at Rome:

> Therefore, since we are justified by faith, we have peace with God through our Lord Jesus Christ.
>
> (Romans 5.1)

Several times he reminds the recipients of his letters that peace is an essential aspect of the Christian life, a fruit of the Spirit, a result of our relationship with God through Christ. The writer of the letter to the Ephesians goes further than this and calls the Gospel itself 'the Gospel of Peace' (6.15) and states that Christ 'is our peace' (2.14).

The quest for peace of mind and heart is there in all religions and is the great benefit held out by techniques of meditation and contemplation. The Christian emphasis is that this inner peace, which is in essence the union of human wills with the divine will, is present in Christ, not to be earned but to be received as a gift. This does not make the mystical quest null and void. On the contrary, the path of prayer is a way of receiving, at deeper and deeper levels of our being, what is offered in Christ. Nor is it to be seen apart from the sacramental receiving of that gift in Holy Communion. When Christians receive the sacrament there is a Holy Union, a Holy Communion. This union is the union of the divine and the human which those 'in Christ' share.

This inner peace can be grasped even in the midst of turmoil and conflict. For it is a peace that nothing can destroy. But it is not an alternative to Shalom or an attempt to escape the obligation to bring Shalom to bear on the whole of human existence. Shalom, in its fullness, lies in the future, for it is that union of all things with the creator which nothing can destroy. That union can be received now at a personal level. However, it is not an alternative to the whole but a sliver of the whole; a handhold in the inner life on what one day will embrace all life. Inner peace is a foretaste of what one day will include the whole of social, economic and political existence; and inner peace carries with it an obligation to work for the whole of which it is a part.

> We beseech thee, O Lord our God, to set the peace of heaven within the hearts of men, that it may bind the nations also in a covenant which cannot be broken, through Jesus Christ our Lord.[5]

The God of Peace

Peace in all forms, Shalom, Pax and inner, comes from God and is a gift of God. Peace is an essential characteristic of his being and it is from that being that we receive peace. Many times in Paul's writings he refers to 'the peace of God' or 'the peace from God'.

> Now may the Lord of peace himself give you peace at all times in all ways.
>
> (2 Thessalonians 3.16)

This does not refer only to inner peace. The Hebrew scriptures are no less clear in their affirmation that Pax, peace with neighbours, peace within the borders and at the borders, is a gift of God; and so of course is Shalom.

This raises again the general problem of the relationship between divine gift and human effort. This question is outside the scope of this report but here as elsewhere they should not be seen as mutually exclusive. Our peace-making is nothing less than the gift of God in and through us. The gift of peace we pray for is also the peace we work for. We are conscious of needing the gift because we know that of ourselves we can do nothing that is lasting.

> *Nisi Dominus* Except the Lord build the house; their labour is but lost that build it.
>
> (Psalm 127.1)

A Single Peace

Shalom, Pax and Inner tranquillity seem very different forms of peace. Yet within a Christian perspective they are integrally related to one another, as this ancient prayer makes clear:

> O God, who wouldest fold both heaven and earth in a single peace; let the design of thy great love lighten upon the wastes of our wraths and sorrows; and give peace to thy church, peace among nations, peace in our dwellings and peace in our heart; through thy Son our saviour Jesus Christ.[6]

As already considered inner peace is to be seen as a fragmentary anticipation of that Shalom which will one day embrace all things; a receiving in personal and at first inward terms of what will one day include all that is social and outward. Pax too, although it contains elements in it derived from coercion and the fear of the consequences of certain actions, is not unrelated to Shalom, for Pax too will include elements in it based on free consent, on mutual goodwill and the common good. Nevertheless, there are clearly special difficulties in thinking about the relationship between Pax and Shalom. These stem from the fact that in the state of affairs where Shalom takes full effect power relationships have been transcended but in the world in which we live they are the fundamental feature of relationships between organised groups. Before that relationship is considered further however, some mention must be made of the role of conflict in life and of the notion of false peace, which figures in the scriptures so prominently.

The Role of Conflict and the Exposure of False Peace

Most human beings shy away from conflict and there is a tendency to think that conflict is incompatible with the Christian life. In heaven it may be different but conflict is a fundamental and proper part of earthly existence. It is through the possibility of conflict that individuals and groups have opportunity to share their perspective, state their concern and work for their interest. Without the possibility of conflict between different perspectives, concerns and interests this freedom would not exist.

There is of course both proper and improper conflict. There is the improper conflict that springs from the hearts of those out to make trouble; which springs from the malice that can wreck any human system. That is why, on a Christian view, practical arrangements for the ordering of human affairs can never be entirely separated from *ascesis*, the inner discipline or purifying of the heart, which seeks to ensure that those affairs are managed by people of goodwill rather than malevolence.

Then there is the improper conflict which, born of a mixture of legitimate self-interest and improper pride, seeks to resolve a particular conflict by force of arms when other means of redress are still open. It is part of the rationale of a democratic system that it enables conflicts to be resolved without resort to violence, through law and Parliament; which makes possible even the change of governments without recourse to violence.

Within the international order there do not yet exist totally adequate mechanisms for the peaceful resolution of conflict. The

United Nations recognises this both in its support of peace-keeping forces and in its recognition of the right of self-defence as a last resort. When a nation defends itself against external aggression or when it rises up against an occupying power then that conflict, though tragic, is proper under the present conditions of human existence. Failure to resist or to take the necessary steps to offer adequate resistance can be a failure of responsibility; an acquiescence in a false peace.

There is peace of a kind to be had by shutting the heart and mind to all that disturbs. Clearly this kind of peace in a cocoon should have no part in the Christian life. Such a peace is to be had only by selling our birthright as human beings, as Wilfred Owen makes clear in his poem 'Insensibility':

> But cursed are dullards whom no cannon stuns
> that they should be as stones.
> Wretched are they, and mean
> with paucity that never was simplicity.
> By choice they made themselves immune
> to pity and whatever mourns in men.[7]

There is a false peace to be had by accepting social injustice. When Martin Luther King was in prison a group of white pastors wrote to him urging him to stop disturbing the peace. He wrote back that 'Peace is not the absence of tension but the presence of justice.' In South Africa many prayers are offered for peace on her borders. But the sons or grandsons of black members of those congregations where such prayers are offered may be on the other side of those borders praying for a peace that is the fruit of justice. That striving for justice is a greater contribution to Shalom than premature attempts to achieve a reconciliation based on injustice.

> For from the least to the greatest of them,
> every one is greedy for unjust gain;
> and from prophet to priest,
> every one deals falsely.
> They have healed the wound of my people lightly,
> saying 'Peace, peace',
> When there is no peace.
>
> (Jeremiah 6.13–14. See also 8.11.)

This kind of peace is likened to daubing over cracks with white-wash. The destruction of such whitewashed buildings is inevitable:

> Because, yea, because, they have misled my people, saying, 'Peace', when there is no peace; and because when the people build a wall, these prophets daub it with whitewash: say to those who daub it with whitewash that it shall fall!
>
> (Ezekiel 13.10–11)

When Jesus came he brought the Shalom of the Kingdom of God. His birth was preceded by that of John the Baptist who came to prepare the way for one who would 'guide our feet into the way of peace'. (Luke 1.79)

At the birth of the Messiah the heavens rang with the song

> 'Glory to God in the highest, and on earth peace among men with whom he is pleased.'
>
> (Luke 2.14)

The disciples when they were sent out were directed to bring this peace to the houses where they were staying.

> Whatever house you enter, first say 'Peace be to this house.' And if a son of peace is there, your peace shall rest upon him; but if not it shall return to you.
>
> (Luke 10.5–6. See also Matthew 10.12–13.)

This peace, this Shalom of God, which broke into the world in the person of Jesus, came into conflict with the corrupt practices and unjust structures of human existence. There could be no easy accommodation with the peace of men; conflict was inevitable. So we get the terrible words:

> Do not think that I have come to bring peace on earth; I have not come to bring peace but a sword.
>
> (Matthew 10.34)

This brought anguish to the Son of God.

> And when he drew near and saw the city he wept over it, saying 'would that even today you knew the things that make for peace! But now they are hid from your eyes.'
>
> (Luke 19.41–42)

The Christian vocation is not only to preach the peace of Christ but to expose false peace, a peace based on insensitivity and complacency; a peace rooted in injustice and suppression of dissent. Exposing this false peace inevitably leads to conflict. But this conflict is an essential prelude to that Shalom which is the product of justice; of a right relationship with God that is reflected in right relationships between human beings, not on domination but mutual respect and equality of concern.

Shalom and Pax

It has already been suggested that Shalom and Pax are not unrelated to one another, for in all forms of Pax there will be an element, however minimal, of free consent. Nevertheless, in this world there will often be a tension between them, because Pax makes use of, and rightly makes use of, elements of coercion to maintain order both within a state and between states. This tension is inescapable for the Christian, because in one sense the Kingdom of God has already come and yet its full consummation lies in the future. The rule of God has already taken form in this world in the life, death and resurrection of Jesus Christ. Yet Christians live between the times: between the time of his rising and his coming again. Every line of the New Testament reflects this tension. The presence of this tension is not due to a 'sell-out' to worldliness. On the contrary, it is a recognition of the legitimate, that is, God-given, claims of civil society. So long as God wills human life to continue, he wills human communities, for human beings are essentially social; there can be no human personhood without social life. This social life needs political structures and so long as life continues Christians have a duty, along with other citizens, of maintaining a just and peaceable order. As Augustine put it:

> Thus, the heavenly City, so long as it is wayfaring on earth, not only makes use of earthly peace but fosters and actively pursues along with other human beings a common platform in regard to all that concerns our purely human life.[8]

Ultimately a Christian's allegiance is to the one, undivided and unified will of God. Nevertheless, searching for this will in the actual conditions under which we live, a Christian becomes conscious of two sets of claims upon him, not just one. There are the claims that arise out of our membership of civil society and there are the claims derived from the demands of the Kingdom of God. The first set of claims, of 'our station and its duties', to use the phrase of A. D. Lindsay, is referred to by Paul in Romans 13 (see the comment on this passage in Chapter 3). The other set of claims, that posed by the challenge of perfection, finds its most sublime expression in the Sermon on the Mount. Until the Kingdom of God comes in its fullness, that is so long as God wills human societies to exist under sinful conditions, these two sets of claims will live in necessary tension with one another. Nevertheless, they are integrally related, that is, Shalom bears upon Pax in a number of ways.

First, Shalom provides a true vision, an ultimate standard in the light of which the whole of human life is to be seen and judged. It reveals our present forms of peace for what they are, sometimes a false peace based on injustice, sometimes Pax, a compromise made necessary by a sinful world.

Secondly, Shalom presents us with an obligation to work for this vision and to express it so far as we can under the conditions of sinful finite existence. Mention was made earlier of the way in which religion can be used to disguise and justify the drive to dominate others. But Christian faith keeps before us the vision of true religion, which works to break down the barriers which divide us and bring about reconciliation between warring parties, a theme which is explored in relation to East-West relations in Chapter 10. It has been argued earlier that in the world as we know it Pax may depend upon power being checked by countervailing power. But again, Christian faith bids us lift up our eyes to the horizon of the cross, where all human power is humbled before the self-emptying love of God. So we are called to work for reconciliation, even at great cost to ourselves. Such work is not in vain. For it is possible for there to be anticipations and signs of Shalom.

Inner peace can be such a sign. The commitment of a community to justice and reconciliation can be such a sign. The life of a Church built on a mutual forgiveness that is rooted in the forgiveness of God can be such a sign.

Shalom presents us with a vision of peace and justice that impels us to work for a transformed world. Not just in the inner life or the Church but in the whole complex of human political relationships, we look for and work for, transformation. Our prayer will be:

Show us, good Lord,
the peace we should seek,
the peace we must give,
the peace we can keep,
the peace we must forgo,
and the peace you have given
in Jesus Christ our Lord.[9]

Summary

There are three distinct but interrelated aspects to the Christian tradition on peace, Shalom, Pax and inner peace which together give us the Christian doctrine. We will need each of their distinctive contributions as we move on in this report to the complexities of the task of making and keeping peace in our present world. To focus on one of these aspects to the exclusion of the others would distort our view. Together they affirm the necessary persistent political work of seeking to prevent war and violence and to enable peace to be sustained. The outworking of this Christian concept of peace needs to take place in the management of the historic divisions of power, interest and ideology which lie behind the present East-West divide. In Chapter 9 we will look at the meaning of these themes for détente and reconciliation and in Chapter 10 at their outworking in the management of contemporary East-West relationships. In the search for Pax we are sustained both by the inward strength of purpose given by the experience of peace in our lives and by the vision of Shalom for which we all long and strive.

Footnotes

[1] Michael Howard, 'The Concept of Peace'. *Encounter*, Dec. 1983, Vol. LXI, No. 4.

[2] *Ibid.*

[3] J. F. Powers, the American writer of humorous short stories, describes in one of them life in a Roman Catholic rectory from the standpoint of the cat. As the cat put it at one point:

> Unfortunately, it is naked power that counts most in any rectory and as things stand now, I am safe only so long as Father Malt retains it here.

J. F. Powers, 'Death of a Favorite', *The Presence of Grace*. The Hogarth Press, 1977, p.152.

[4] William Wordsworth, 'The Excursion' in *The Poems*, Vol. 11. Penguin, 1977, p.152.

[5] *The Cuddesdon Office Book*. OUP, 1961, p.179.

[6] *After the Third Collect*, ed. Eric Milner-White. Mowbray.

[7] Wilfred Owen, 'Insensibility' in *War Poems and Others*, ed. Dominic Hibbern. Chatto and Windus, 1975, p.89.

[8] Augustine, *The City of God*, Book XIX, chap. 17. Augustine does not use pax in the same sense that it is defined in this chapter.

[9] Prayer adopted by the Corrymeela Community in Northern Ireland and originally published in *Contemporary Prayers for Public Worship*, ed. Caryl Micklem. SCM.

2
Christian Hope in a Nuclear Age

Biblical Hope

We rejoice in our hope of sharing the glory of God.

(Romans 5.2)

Joy and hope were distinguishing marks of the early Christian believers. All the New Testament writings are filled with a sense of hope; but perhaps the letter to the Christians at Rome expresses the importance of hope most clearly:

Hope does not disappoint us because God's love has been poured into our hearts through the Holy Spirit.

(Romans 5.5)

It is the gift of the Spirit, renewing and transforming human life, which arouses hope in us—hope for that final sharing in the divine glory which is discerned in the ascension of the Lord. Yet Christian hope is not for some sort of individual glory. It is not even for some particular group of people, like members of the Church. On the contrary:

the creation itself will be set free from its bondage to decay and obtain the glorious liberty of the children of God. We know that the whole creation has been groaning in travail together until now . . . for in this hope we were saved.

(Romans 8.21–24)

Christian hope is for the liberation of the world from its bondage to decay. It looks for a new heaven and earth, a new age—and it founds its hope on the experience of the risen appearances of Christ, and on the experience of the power of the Holy Spirit in the new communities of disciples.

It is essential to set Christian hope in the whole context of biblical revelation, which claims to declare the will of the Creator for the creation. Throughout the Hebrew Bible, God gives commands to the people of Israel which point them to the need for justice and mercy in society. The Torah, the law of God of Israel, declared through Moses, is not concerned solely with religious or ritual affairs, or with an area of private and inward morality. It is concerned with the existence of a just society, obedient to God in all things and imitating God in the ways of justice and truth, a society characterised by Shalom. The revelation of God to the prophets gives a vision of a new society, in which injustice and suffering will be vanquished. It gives God's own promise that such a society will come to be. For the Hebrew prophets teach with quite distinctive force that the God who makes himself known to them has a purpose for the world. That purpose will be realised; and human beings are given the responsibility to help realise it. The purpose is a society of peace and justice; and salvation, or liberation, consists in the existence of such a society, in which all will be free from oppression and hatred. (See the discussion of Shalom in Chapter 1.)

Jesus came, so the Gospel writers declare, not to negate that vision, that command and that promise, but to fulfil them in a new and higher way (cf. Matt. 5.17–20). His first recorded preaching was the proclamation that God's rule or Kingdom was at hand (Matt. 4.17). Not only that, it was present in his own person, and was discernible in his works of healing and forgiveness:

> If it is by the spirit of God that I cast out demons, then the Kingdom of God has come upon you.
>
> (Matt. 12.28)

Both Jesus' teaching and his actions were concerned with the Kingdom, and those who gathered around him looked for the dawning of that Kingdom at any time. What they looked for was the fulfilment of the ancient prophetic hope of Israel—the dawning of the day of the Lord, when evil would be destroyed and peace would flourish on earth. Their hope was not individual and purely spiritual—it was social and material, a hope for the renewal of the earth.[1]

And yet the cataclysm did not come. Imperial Rome, irritated beyond endurance by rebellious Israel, obliterated the Jewish nation completely. Jesus, the prophet of the Kingdom, died as a common criminal or alleged political agitator. But the world did not end, and Jesus did not return on the clouds with glory. The little band of Jesus' disciples should have died out quietly, their dream shattered, their hope abandoned. One of the most remarkable facts of world history is that they proceeded to carry their gospel of hope throughout the whole earth, and to build a Church which outlived many empires. How could such hope survive and grow? There are two main reasons. First, they realised from early on that their time-scale might well not be God's. So the second letter of Peter says:

> With the Lord one day is as a thousand years, and a thousand years as one day.
>
> (2 Peter 3.8)

It is not for us to know the times and seasons; so:

> if we hope for what we do not see, we wait for it with patience.
>
> (Romans 8.25)

The early Christians did not give up hope for a renewed earth; but they made no claim to know when or how it would come about— and were content to leave that in the providence of God.

Secondly, and more important, early Christian hope was founded on the belief that God had already poured his love into their hearts, and that

> nothing in all creation will be able to separate us from the love of God in Christ Jesus.
>
> (Romans 8.39)

They believed that their feeling of the power of the Spirit within them showed that renewal had already begun, just as they had seen in Jesus the beginning of something quite new in human history. Their hope was for the completion of this renewal, not for something entirely different. And the basis of their hope was the very love of God which they felt so powerfully working within them. A God of such love would realise his purposes— and those purposes would fulfil and perfect human lives and human society and indeed the whole created order. But again, how and when this would come about was quite outside the power of human prediction or understanding.

What this means is that the heart and reality of Christian faith is rooted in something that happens now, as the risen power of

Christ is made present within the community of faith. Christians are not merely waiting for something good to happen in future, with a sort of desperate optimism. They find their lives being transformed in the present, by the Holy Spirit who makes God's love real to them:

> The time is coming *and now is*, when true worshippers worship the Father in spirit and truth.
>
> (John 4.23)

It is that present transformation of human lives which is the strength and mainstay of Christian believing—and that strength is the work of the Spirit of God.

From the first, nonetheless, and as an essential part of faith, Christians have looked for the completion of this transformation, for the liberation of the earth, for the coming of Christ in glory, 'at the right hand of power' (Mark 14.62). The 'mystery of faith' which is proclaimed in the Anglican liturgy is that 'Christ has died; Christ is risen; Christ will come again'. That hope for the *Parousia*, the fully realised presence of Christ in all the world, is central to Christian hope. But it is difficult for many to come to terms with, when our view of the universe, its vastness in time and space, is so different from that of the first Christians.

All who read the first three Gospels and the letters to the Thessalonians know the language about 'the end of the age' which is to be found there—the great tribulation, the final battle with evil, and then the darkening of sun, moon and stars and the return of Christ in the clouds, gathering his elect from every nation, before the final Day of Judgement. All who read the great prophets of the Old Testament know the heavily symbolic nature of such language, as it is used to apply to political and social events concerned with the exile and return of the Israelites.[2] There is by no means universal agreement among Christians on how much of the language is symbolic, or on just what it symbolises. On the one hand, there are those who expect a literal abrupt end to the planet earth, not too far in the future.[3] On the other hand, there are those, like the great biblical scholars C. H. Dodd and G. B. Caird, who regard the language of the Apocalypse as an almost wholly symbolic and dramatised picture which either depicts events which occurred with the birth of the Church ('realised eschatology'),[4] or foreshortens aeons of earthly history into a brief time, using conventions and poetic devices alien to present-day modes of thought, and therefore very difficult for us to interpret.[5]

The mainstream Christian Churches, and the Church of England in particular, have never required assent to any particular interpretation of Apocalyptic writing. The most important question is to ask what these passages *mean*—whether and in what way they are symbolic. The Bible itself gives no answer to that question. One has to make an interpretation based on a knowledge of similar texts, on Church tradition and on general theological grounds. All Christians have to do this, however certain they may be of the particular tradition they accept.

There is a general consensus among Anglican scholars that, however much symbolism there is in the biblical language, three beliefs are central to full Christian hope. First, there will be a full realisation of God's purpose for the universe, and a final defeat of evil. Secondly, all human beings will share in this consummation, and not only those who happen to be alive at the time. Thirdly, Christ will be fully revealed to all as the mediator between humanity and divinity in his own person, the saviour of the world.

We cannot picture what this will be like, or how it will happen. God has not provided an exact timetable and programme of events. Indeed, it is a form of heresy—the Millenialist heresy—to claim to have such a timetable. Those who hold it usually leave the main body of the Christian Church, and tend to wither away as their timetables are shown to be false. They have failed to remember the words of Jesus:

> of that day and hour no one knows, not the angels in heaven nor the Son.
>
> (Mark 13.32)

The same Gospel records Jesus as saying:

> Watch, therefore, for you do not know when the Lord of the house comes.
>
> (Mark 13.35)

Even if we reject secret knowledge of divine timetables, Christians must always live, not in fear of divine judgement, but in eager anticipation of the full revelation of divine glory. It is wrong to think of the *Parousia* as so far in the future that it does not immediately concern us. It should colour our thoughts and hopes now, giving an urgency and vitality to our actions. However, at just this point a terrible misunderstanding of Christian doctrine can occur, in an age when we can destroy the earth by nuclear catastrophe. Some have suggested, however incredible it seems, that God wills a nuclear holocaust, as his way of ending the world.[6] So we may welcome it; or at least fail to work with all our might to prevent it.

That is not only a misunderstanding; it is blasphemy. If the earth is destroyed, that will not destroy the Christian hope. But if it is destroyed through our collusion, then we ally ourselves with the forces of destruction, and exclude ourselves from that hope. There are major differences between the Christian hope for a new age, and the terrible thought that a nuclear holocaust might be in accordance with God's will.[7] First, the Bible speaks of a 'new heaven and a new earth'; it is speaking of a renewal of the whole cosmos; it would be misleading to identify this hope with the destruction of one small planet, as though such destruction would somehow accomplish the rolling up of the stars. The identification of the *Parousia* with the end of the planet earth is almost certainly mistaken, a point which is developed in Chapter 8. Secondly, the great battles of the biblical Apocalypse are battles primarily between supernatural powers. The elect do not fight; and they are certainly not encouraged to think that by taking up weapons they can bring in the new age. One cannot transfer these scenes of a war in heaven to the earthly plane directly; and whatever they symbolise of the war against evil, it is not that human beings should take up arms against it. This connects with a third point, that the message of the cross is that evil cannot be defeated by the exercise of power. The world is God's creation, and we are called to be messengers of reconciliation in it, not its destroyers. Finally the crucified God is not a god who wills evil. He may permit humans to bring it on themselves and on each other; he may show justice in his dealings with evil. But the God revealed in Christ, who gives himself to the uttermost to save even one sinner, is not one who wills that responsible creatures should knowingly cause the deaths of millions of innocent lives. Thus, whatever the right interpretation of the biblical images of the last battle which eradicates evil from God's creation, it is naive, mistaken and dangerous to take them as any sort of vindication of policies which may, by our compliance, lead to the deaths of vast numbers of innocent children of God and to the intentional destruction of a world that God has made.

We can see from this that Christian hope is not for something quite specific and clearly describable. It is for an almost wholly unimaginable future, for a sort of life incorruptible and strong which is beyond our present clouded thoughts (1 Cor. 15.42–43). Yet it is hope, for it is concerned with an amplification and completion of the good that God has shown us so far. And it carries with it an obligation to strive to realise the goods of creation, even if they seem to come to nothing. The first Christians were, at their best, glad to be martyrs for their faith; their hope was not defeated by temporal failures and apparent defeats. They had too strong a faith in the cross to think that such defeats would never come yet they believed that, if defeats came, they were not the final word. God has the power to realise his purpose for us, despite all that evil can do.

Hope and Human Action

This point carries another implication for Christian hope. It is right to aim at what one hopes for by appropriate action. But if one hopes for union with God, and for the achievement of God's purposes for the world, there are some sorts of action which are ruled out. God has given us the pattern of our action in the life of Jesus; and we know that it ended, as a publicly observable life, on the cross. So the Christian hope, and the Christian vision of society, must be one that is prepared, if necessary, to face and endure a sort of cross. The Kingdom will not come by violence; and though we must strive to bring in the Kingdom, there will be some things we cannot do to bring it in.[8]

Christian and Marx-Leninist Hopes

It is in this way that Christian hope for the future differs from the hope of Marx-Leninism, even though that philosophy has some interesting parallels with Hebrew prophetic tradition. It must be noted that the writings of Marx himself are not to be identified with the Soviet form of Marx-Leninism, and they are susceptible of a number of interpretations and revisions. There may be strong disagreements between some forms of Christian social teaching and particular social systems which claim to be Marx-Leninist. But it need not follow that all forms of Christianity are opposed to all forms of Marxism. In fact, many fascinating parallels exist between the two systems of thought, each of which is itself capable of being given differing emphases. Marx uses many concepts typical of the Hebraic tradition—a historical purpose; a goal of social justice; a prophetic condemnation of oppression; the role of an 'elect' in foreshadowing the new age; and the battle with forces of exploitation which will lead to the dawn of the new age. Marx believed that the processes of history were moving inevitably towards the existence of a just society, in which all human beings could achieve true freedom and self-realisation. It is important to remember that Marxism is committed to the realisation of a just society on earth; so that it is committed against any policy which would lead to the extermination of all life on earth rather than give up some favoured ideology. Marx is committed to hope for a human future; and the roots for this view are to be found in the tradition of Hebrew prophecy.

It has been plausibly argued that Marx was greatly influenced in the formulation of some of his ideas by the biblical tradition.[9] Certainly the German philosopher Hegel, many of whose notions Marx used, even while reacting against them in some respects, considered himself to be giving a philosophical exposition of Christian faith. It is thus no accident that one can point to a number of mutual influences between some sorts of Marxian and Christian thought, which may suggest the possibility of future developments in both of a creative and fruitful sort. It may be that failures of institutional Christianity have helped to give Marxism power; and liberation theology expresses a form of biblical interpretation which has been stimulated by the influence of Marx. It would be quite wrong to pretend that Marxism and Christian faith have no important differences. But it would also be wrong to write off possibilities of future development and change which may make present animosities seem irrelevant—to be open to such possibilities of transformation is a proper part of Christian hope.[10]

From a Christian point of view, three major differences seem at present to exist between mainstream forms of Christianity and most Marxist views. First, human liberation for Marx is to be achieved without repentance and faith in God, without that transformation of character which Christians believe can only be brought about by the redeeming power of Christ. So it must pin its faith on human effort alone, usually rejecting any idea of the need for redemption by a higher spiritual power. Secondly, Marxism has no higher law or power by which human societies can be judged. The human is the measure of all things. So there is no providence which can realise goodness despite human failure; no eternal law which forbids doing evil that good may come; and no sense of being under judgement and accepted through grace alone. Thirdly, Marxism claims to be based on a strictly scientific and materialist view of history. Even though the term 'science' may be given a very wide interpretation, for Marxists, there remains the difference that, on the Christian view, the future is not predictable by a scientific study of the laws of nature alone. For the future is always open to the action of a personal God who responds as he will (though always in judgement and mercy) to the actions of creatures. For Christians, there is a personal, moral and creatively free dimension to history which makes it always elusive to strictly scientific prediction and control.

These differences may not prove to be absolute obstacles to further developments of understanding between the two systems of thought. But it is as well to have them clearly in view when seeking to understand the ideologies which are most widely accepted by the competing nuclear powers. An important part of the process of peacemaking is to achieve a clear, correct and undistorted view of the basic beliefs and values which are at issue. Many differences may need to be accepted. But it is important for Christians to recognise that they share a common hope with Marxists for a just society of truly free persons. This is in itself a sign of hope in a world which tends to be seen as divided between a 'Christian West' and a 'Marxist East'. Such a view ignores the many other world-groupings which exist, perhaps especially the North-South division between the richer and poorer nations. And it may underestimate the possibilities for quite radical change which exist in international relations. It may be unduly myopic to think that the Christian-Marxist split is unchangeable or even likely to endure for a very long period of time in its present form.

Whatever possibilities of hope exist in international relations, however, Christians must confess that their hope is primarily in God; 'Thou, O Lord, art my hope' (Ps. 71.5). That must give a special character to Christian hope. It is not mere optimism about the future, or some sort of Utopian wishful thinking. It is founded on the disclosure of the love of God in Jesus Christ, and it requires commitment to love as its first principle.

Christian hope can therefore face the defeat of its plans and efforts with patience. A faith which is founded on acceptance of a resurrection which comes by way of the cross and death cannot look for a natural and painless transition to the just society. It cannot be undermined by worldly failure, and it should never be misled into claiming worldly success. The resolute action without anxious attachment for which Jesus calls (Matt. 6.25) is only possible when we accept in faith that our acts will find fulfilment, but do not look for the fulfilment in immediate social change. Christian hope requires us to measure our political acts by standards and norms higher than those of expediency or practicality; yet nonetheless seek to realise those standards as far as possible within the conditions and constraints of our own time.

In the face of the constant evidence of human sin and failure, it is tempting perhaps to make the Christian hope completely other-worldly or to place its realisation so far in the future that it makes little difference to present action. But this would be to miss entirely that note of 'eager expectation' (Romans 8.19) which marked the faith of Jesus' disciples. Jesus taught his disciples to keep watchful, for the end of all things was already present and at hand in his person. To grasp the teaching of Jesus on this point one needs to speak both of the fulfilment of all things, at the consummation of God's purpose for creation, when all things on heaven and earth shall be made one in Christ (Eph. 1.10); and of the way in which each moment of history is already related to its fulfilment in the eternal being of God. The 'End of all things' is not some remote final moment of time—just as the creation is not some remote first moment of time. The Christian doctrine of creation sees every moment as a new creation at the hand of God. Every moment depends wholly for its existence on the Eternal Being which is its source. In the same way, the Christian doctrine of salvation sees every moment as returning to, being caught up in and transfigured by, that Eternal Being which is its goal. The present is not to be lost for ever, as a mere means to some far future perfect state. Each moment is *part* of that consummation, and can be seen as such when it is seen from the standpoint of the completed pattern of all things, from the standpoint of eternity. Thus the end is present in every time as the openness to eternity of each moment. Every moment has an eternal significance, as the end of all things breaks into every present. Christian hope must have that element of keen watchfulness and eager anticipation; for it is the discernment of God's future in the present moment, of a future consummation which is not remote and far away, but which is the completion of our present actions and experiences, seen in their eternal perspective.[11]

In later chapters we consider some of the hopeful possibilities that are present in Soviet-American relationships. These can be discussed in purely secular terms. From a theological point of view, however, they are part of God's transformed future anticipated in the present. This is because Christian hope for the Kingdom of God embraces the whole of human existence, including superpower relationships. And although Christian hope finds its fulfilment beyond the spatio-temporal order, it is to be worked for, and signs of its presence can be seen, on this earth.

Christian hope, then, rests upon the conviction that reality is opened up to something new in the event of Christ and the birth of the Church. It is opened to the love of God, from which nothing can separate us. There is no final closing off of human history from God and so from a future of healing. Christian hope does not mean that we can remain as we are, with our desires and goals unchanged and fixed on material assets or the passions of self-aggrandisement, and yet be somehow assured that nothing bad will happen to us. On the contrary, it is only insofar as we begin to change or be changed, that hope comes to be formed in us as the anticipation of the full realisation of that unbroken relation to God which is given to us in Christ. This is not an empty Utopianism, trusting human nature or a friendly anthropomorphic providence to produce an agreeable or painless outcome; it is a belief which requires a change of character and a turning from self towards God; it is in this sense that the Christian believes that 'all things work together for good to those who love God' (Romans 8.28). Goodness will not be defeated. There is never room, in the Christian vision, for despair, for the belief that God's purpose will be finally frustrated. Yet Christians should be fully aware of the dark possibilities of a world sundered from God by sin, where risk and self-sacrifice may be called for, as the way to fulfilment.

Hope in a Nuclear Age

Might this not lead to a sort of passive or escapist piety, which leaves the world to end in ruin, if it so chooses? At precisely this point, the doctrines of the incarnation and resurrection lay a distinctive emphasis on the historical, the material and the particular, which distinguishes it from all neo-Platonic themes, however much they have been used in the formulation of classical Christian theology. Mysterious as it is, the doctrine of the resurrection of the body encapsulates the idea that human personality is to be fulfilled, not negated, in the attainment of the final good. Thus it is what we have actually done and achieved that will be fulfilled, and what we have suffered and undergone that will be transfigured by its inclusion in a wider life. If God became flesh, then flesh has been made for ever holy, in all its particularity and even idiosyncracies of nature.

Christian hope is rooted in this world, even if it is not to be wholly fulfilled within this world. That means it has a double aspect, if it is to be rightly understood. On the one hand it cannot be defeated by a failure to achieve full realisation in the world. On the other hand, it cannot be achieved by a mere deferment to some future life. It is a hope for this world; but not for this world only.

And it is not a hope for some purely spiritual flight from the material; it is rather a hope for the transfiguration of the material, to make it a sacrament of the divine.

That means that the Church must encourage its members to work actively for peace, as the building up of trust and community, especially among those between whom there has been or still is enmity. It must encourage them to take risks in the direction of self-sacrifice for the sake of peace. And it must counsel them never to despair, to say that no good is possible or to fail to see present action as contributing to future good. Perhaps the words of Martin Luther make a good motto for the character of Christian hope: 'If I knew the world would end tomorrow, I would plant a tree.' In this spirit the Church must unceasingly proclaim the hope which is placed before us as 'the anchor of our souls' (Heb. 6.19), so that we may practise that eager expectation of the manifestation of God's glory which fills the Christian's life with joy and peace (Romans 15.13).

Is there anything which the Christian doctrine of hope has to say specifically to the nuclear age? It is undoubtedly true that the large-scale possession of huge stocks of nuclear weapons (and also the knowledge we possess of biological warfare weapons) puts the human race in a new situation. For the first time, it is possible that relatively few human actions might eliminate all human life from the planet. Even if that does not happen, it is possible to kill and maim vast numbers of innocent people over generations, and adversely to affect those as yet unborn. Thus the potential for destruction, and the deaths of people quite uninvolved in any conflict, are of unprecedented proportions. Moreover, the whole matter of warfare is called in question in a more radical way, because war involving a full-scale nuclear war would be unwinnable by either side. One is no longer able to calculate the possibility of obtaining some good for oneself out of such a conflict. Or, even if one tries such a calculation, there is a substantial risk that a nuclear exchange will get out of control, and unleash consequences one could not possibly justify in a less heated moment. Then there is the fact that only a very small number of people have the capacity to unleash such a war—so that the most immense destructive power is put into the hands of a tiny number of people, who exercise that power in conditions of the strictest secrecy. And, perhaps worst of all, when a government is in the position of being prepared to do absolutely anything to defend its own system, moral vision is corrupted at its root. There is nothing worth defending, if it requires being prepared to do absolutely anything to defend it. To say otherwise from a Christian point of view, is to lead to a spiritual blindness, a dullness of the moral imagination, which undermines the very values one is pretending to support.

Of course, the calculation of nuclear strategists are much more subtle than all this may suggest. Yet the fact remains that all the terrible possibilities outlined here are no longer idle fantasies. There is always some risk that they may be actualised. In such a world, the sense of individual powerlessness can assume huge proportions. A belief in the inevitability of destruction, sooner or later, can take hold. It may even come to be thought that, in such a situation of doomed helplessness, no moral considerations are worth taking seriously any more. Moral sincerity is undermined by a belief, well or ill-founded, that the moral guardians of one's society are prepared to go to any lengths to avoid backing down. Moral sensitivity is undermined by the perception that the subtlest ethical thinking can apparently end by being prepared to destroy the innocent wholesale. In such an age, fear, anxiety and despair are constant threats which plague human beings; and the more sensitive and reflective one is, the more they threaten to paralyse the human will.

The Christian gospel does not assure everyone that it will never happen (see Chapter 8). The earliest Christians were prepared for the world to end in destruction; and the possibility of catastrophe has always been present for individuals and whole societies of men and women. Hope may decay into indifference in a world which is apparently irredeemably hostile and locked into a self-destructive conflict. Slowly it decays into an indifference which kills all creative action and moral endeavour. Christian hope is a bulwark against this decay. For it rests on the faith that God is creator still. The future is always open to the unexpectedness of his touch, and his ultimate purpose is beyond defeat. So one can never rest content with present conflicts, or suppose that they are beyond change and reconciliation. One can never acquiesce in doing evil that good may come, in deliberately killing the innocent to keep one's territory. One can never give up hope for God's world; or, on the other hand, suppose that the worst human folly and wickedness signals the failure of his creative design. One can never give up the vision of a renewed earth, which calls us to seek to realise it so far as we may, and which promises that:

> the earth will be filled with the knowledge of the glory of the Lord, as the waters cover the sea.
>
> (Hab. 2.14)

It is because the nuclear age poses a threat of planetary proportions that the Christian hope of a renewed world speaks to it with particular relevance and force. In a world which sometimes seems set upon a course of self-destruction, Paul's prayer remains of peculiar importance. It may appropriately be addressed to a world which asks if there is any hope, and where the source of hope may be found:

> May the God of hope fill you with all joy and peace in believing, so that by the power of the Holy Spirit you may abound in hope.
>
> (Romans 15.13)

Summary

By way of summary, we may say that Christian hope is:

1. based on the love of God with the aim of sharing in his glory. It is not, therefore, purely prudential, concerned for the calculation of practical consequence *alone*;
2. rooted in faith in the providence of God and not, therefore, Utopian with a belief in the gradual improvement of human nature;
3. concerned with the creation of a just society and world of peace. It is not, therefore, individualist in character;
4. seeking the liberation of the whole created order and is not, therefore, other-worldly;

5. placing us under the command of God to seek its realisation now. It is not, therefore, escapist;

6. calling us to be ceaselessly active in love rather than passive in outlook;

7. indestructible, for: 'nothing can separate us from the love of God' (Romans 8.39).

These themes encourage us to engage in the present task of making and keeping the peace in our world however discouraging or adverse the circumstances may be. In Chapter 7 we will be paying particular attention to future possibilities as they appear to us now. In Chapter 8 we will be examining the outworking of Christian concepts of hope in the midst of the debate about deterrence and its associated strategies.

Footnotes

[1] A fuller account can be found in J. Moltmann, *Theology of Hope*. SCM Press, 1967.

[2] Cf. G. B. Caird, *The Language and Imagery of the Bible*. Duckworth, 1980.

[3] An excellent summary of various millenialist theologies is to be found in '*The Meaning of the Millenium' Four Views*. Ed. by R. G. Clouse. IVP, 1977 (USA).

[4] C. H. Dodd, *History and the Gospel*. Nisbet, 1938.

[5] Cf. J. A. T. Robinson, *In the End, God*. Fontana, 1970.

[6] Cf. Hal Lindsay, *The Late Great Planet Earth*. Kingsway, 1978.

[7] Cf. John Austin Baker, 'Theology and Nuclear Weapons', in *King's Theological Review*, Spring, 1983.

[8] The direct killing of the innocent is prohibited in this way. Cf. Richard Harries, *Christianity and War in a Nuclear Age*. Mowbrays, 1986.

[9] S. P. Miranda, *Marx and the Bible*. SCM Press, 1977.

[10] N. L. A. Lash, *A Matter of Hope*. Darton, Longman & Todd, 1981 has a sensitive discussion of Marx from a Christian viewpoint.

[11] Cf. K. Ward, *Reinhold Niebuhr and the Christian Hope*, in *Reinhold Niebuhr and the Issues of Our Time*. Ed. Richard Harries. Mowbrays, 1986.

3
Church, State and Patriotism

1. The Relevance of the Problem

Why should the issue of the Church's relation to state and nation be significant in the discussion of peacemaking? There are at least two reasons. First it is manifest that certain conceptions of the nation-state—its sovereign independence, its authoritative claim upon the loyalty of its citizens—have played a major part both in reflections on the rights and wrongs of war and in the actual conduct of conflict. Secondly, there has come to be a linkage, in recent years, between offers of arms reductions and demands for political reform in the state with which negotiations are being conducted. There is an implicit claim that one state has a right to bring pressure to bear on another sovereign state to shape its policy within its own territory; and this raises some quite complex problems, practical and theoretical. Indeed it has been said by some that the very fact of a negotiating process between East and West carries a concession to the Western model of political conduct, enshrining some ideals of openness, accountability and reformability. This is perhaps controversial; though it is important not to underrate the significance of the Soviet acceptance of open negotiation (not to mention the cautious welcome for on-site verification procedures that they have given) as an acceptance of political conventions not completely alien to what we see as 'Western' modes of operation. But the point about sovereign rights remains a complicated one. In what follows, we shall be looking first at the question of the 'rights' of the sovereign state from a theological perspective, asking what may be said about the limits of its claims, and then at the more specific matter of the kind of pressure that may be properly brought to bear on other states in respect of their internal polity. This will lead us into a wider consideration of the Christian understanding of loyalty and patriotism.

FOUR WAYS OF VIEWING THE STATE

The claims of the nation-state may be put in more or less strong forms. The first and strongest possible view would be in the doctrine that different nations are simply part of God's providential ordering of the world in such a way that a threat to the independence of each nation is an assault on the will of God, a sin as such. This implies not simply that the differentiation of the nations is a good or positive thing, but that it is in some sense fixed by God. This is a view rather seldom heard in international discussions. Not only has its moral credibility been eroded by the practice of Nazi Germany and white South Africa; it is clearly impossible to sustain in the light of even the most minimal historical awareness. It just is not the case that existing sovereign states have anything like the homogeneity of language and ethnic unity required by this view. Most nations are more or less artificial creations in the first instance, and only slowly form for themselves a common identity through history (hence the painful problems faced by 'new' nations in former colonies).

A second and less strong view has been argued which would still have a solid theological component. There are at least two ways in which such a case has been developed. Traditional Catholic theology—typified by a good many modern Papal Encyclicals on social questions—holds that social as well as individual morality is governed by natural law, deriving from a *lex aeterna* in the mind of God. A social order that offends against natural law—a society, for example, ruled by a tyrant or an oligarchy devoted solely to their own interests—would have no legitimacy in the eyes of God. A good many mediaeval theologians believed that something like revolution would be right in such circumstances (some even defended tyrannicide). Similar views were held by Calvinists in the sixteenth and seventeenth centuries. The whole of the 'just war' tradition in Catholic thought presupposes the answerability of state policy to a *lex aeterna*; the rights of a sovereign state to self-defence thus depend upon an assessment of whether or not the state in question is fundamentally at odds with natural justice. It was because he believed the Third Reich to be essentially unjust in this sense that the Austrian peasant Franz Jagerstatter refused military service in the Second World War, and was duly executed.

The other form of this argument to be advanced is far more closely tied to a theology of revelation and conversion and of the claim of the gospel to be the exclusive means of complete human liberation. It is developed particularly in the post-war writings of Karl Barth, where he justifies not a right but a *duty* of self-defence for certain nations in certain circumstances. It may *happen* to be the case that, in a particular confrontation, one party's political life witnesses to values and priorities that leave room for God; that is to say, it does not claim to do what only the Church can do, proclaim the transforming grace of God: it is content with securing those fundamental political decencies (shared access to decision making, to education and welfare, etc.) that make people more fully capable of hearing the word of grace, because they release people from direct material bondage and its concomitant self-contempt or apathy. And the other state involved, presumed to be an aggressor, represents rebelliousness, disorder, idolatry; it claims to offer a total solution to the question of human destiny, and so leaves no room for what the state does not provide. Barth's imagined scenario is an attempted invasion of Switzerland by Nazi Germany. In such circumstances, it is right to defend the threatened order, even if there is little or no possibility of success; not to do so would be to condone idolatry. Defence is a form of witness to the divine limit set to the rights of the state, and thus a summons to the state to be faithful to its determined vocation under God. This is a claim then, which rests on a particular moral or spiritual judgement on one's own nation and its polity, not on any unthinking, irrational loyalty to 'my country, right or wrong'. Barth explicitly leaves open the liberty for the believer not to co-operate, the possibility of Christians making different judgements on their society.

The third version of the state's claim is pragmatically the strongest; theologically it looks to a fairly straightforward reading of Romans 13. Order as such is God's will, a dispensation of providence within which the proper liberties of human beings are secured. For communities to plan their lives and organise their administration, there must be basic communities, fixed points. Law is no terror to the believer, as St Paul says, for it is the necessary presupposition of liberty. There is thus always a *presupposition* in favour of existing order and its nurturing stability. In contrast to the Barthian picture, the state is assumed to be defensible unless very strong reason can be adduced otherwise—not always under question from the eagle-eyed dogmatician. External threat is a menace to this 'nurturing stability'; so there is a presumption in favour of defence, and even in favour of a degree of coercion in securing citizens' co-operation in this task. It is right to maintain sovereignty, even when it rests on no very clear moral legitimation, because it is what sustains the possibility of any kind of political life at all—and that political life is part of God's will for us.

Thus Romans 13.1–6 is frequently cited as a firm statement of the goodness of political authority as such and a clear prohibition against active resistance to authority. This is not quite as obvious as might at first appear. Paul writes in the context of a general discussion of what it is to offer one's entire self to God (Romans 12.1); and a central theme in this discussion is that no Christian is to claim rights and privileges greater than those of other believers or even those of unbelievers. The Christian is thus not outside the ordinary sphere of social restraints. Yet believers also live a life that is in important ways at odds with how the unredeemed world works (12.2). Paul assumes without discussion that this should not be problematic as far as the legal order goes: i.e. he assumes that the divine order observed by Christians is not alien to the bases of good order in society. Ordered society reflects (without knowing it) the order God wills, and disorder—anarchy, rivalry, self-seeking crime—is obviously alien to the will of God. Thus Paul does not here address himself to the difficulties of a situation in which the *de facto* social authority is manifestly promoting *disorder* by sustaining a system that does not discriminate between good and evil (13.3–4). It was obvious to the first Christians—as to Paul himself, it seems, under Nero's persecution—that 'passive resistance', non-co-operation, was not only permissible but obligatory, when authority exceeded its bounds.

Thus the passage certainly supports those who claim that there should normally be a presumption in favour of any system that furthers good order; but it takes for granted that 'good order' is (at least) compatible with the active exercise of Christian discipleship. These verses, therefore, do not support an uncritical attitude to any and every social authority, since the argument for obedience rests on specifically theological grounds for respecting authority —grounds not applicable in absolutely every political situation. What sort or degree of resistance to authority is legitimate is not a question to which the New Testament provides a clear and general answer.

A fourth position exists, diffuse but powerful. Loyalty to the immediate and familiar is instinctive and not really capable of the kind of systematic analysis we have been attempting. We simply *are* born into networks of relation that we have not planned or approved or chosen, and the mere fact of belonging generates an emotional claim. There is nothing wrong in recognising this: indeed it is important to do so, as it is part of recognising our creaturely limitedness. The state is essentially like the family: loyalty is a feeling that cannot be rationalised, and can thus also be represented as a duty that does not need rationalising.

This brief survey may suggest that 'loyalty' in the political realm is a many-faceted notion, and the accusation of disloyalty so frequently levelled in every age of human conflict at those advocating peace is not clear-cut. We may be being asked to be faithful and obedient to the order established by God in creation; or to be committed to a particular account of justice and liberty for the sake of witness to God; or to the fact of order, as the necessary condition of corporate life; or to what is demanded by the plain fact of *belonging*. If, then, we are to be any clearer about the relation between a commitment to peace and loyalty to the state we find ourselves in, we shall need to bear in mind these various senses of loyalty; otherwise we abandon words like loyalty and patriotism to irrationalism and the manipulations of propaganda. We shall return shortly to these issues.

IMPLICATIONS FOR NATION-STATES

The idea of *absolute* sovereign independence for the nation-state or any other empirical political unit is unrealisable (and, for the Christian, idolatrous, insofar as it parodies the self-sufficiency of God). In fact, the conventions of international relations, in some measure reinforced by international law, presuppose that no state is in a position to define terms for its own behaviour quite irrespective of what other states expect of it. A government's claim to be recognised as legitimate, as a partner in the normal amenities of international exchange (diplomatic immunities, passport facilities, regulated currency exchange and trade agreements, conventions about the rights of prisoners of war in time of conflict, etc.) rests not only on *de facto* sovereignty, but on a testable willingness to observe certain decencies. We need to be able to trust each other's promises; and a society whose *internal* life is marked by mistrust or official disinformation makes it harder for other states to take its promises seriously. Its internal practices therefore tend to affect the ease with which it becomes or remains a full partner in international amenities.

Although a 'withdrawal of recognition' of a total kind is very hard to imagine, the principle is well-established that there can be more and less complete forms of recognition and mutual amenity. Some moral considerations, however minimal and pragmatic, enter into questions of what makes an administration legitimate; there is some implicit appeal to an idea of human rights in the conventions of international law, even if only at the level of what it is proper to offer to the citizens of another state in return for what is offered to your own—certain kinds of security, in both peace and war. It is worth noting in passing that, although the Geneva Convention is widely subscribed, the conditions of modern warfare, conventional as much as nuclear, make most historical notions of safeguards in the conduct of war irrelevant. Modern war, especially aerial warfare, makes it practically impossible for any state to give firm guarantees to any other about the safety of non-combatants, once conflict has broken out. This is inevitably productive of deep mistrust and tension; it is perhaps surprising that this has not been even more marked than it has.

It seems to be on the basis of such rather half-formed conceptions of legitimacy that it has come to be assumed that human rights issues may be used as a bargaining chip in negotiations about armaments. There is something of a paradox here. Those in the West most vocal about such issues are usually no less vocal about the need to secure the state against 'blackmail'—i.e. against a vulnerability to pressure that would compromise its sovereignty. However, the readiness to apply pressure to bring about political change elsewhere by linking the military security of another state to its willingness to reform in an acceptable way, implies the qualifying of the claim to an absolute and amoral doctrine of state sovereignty for one's own state. If it is in order to work for change in the USSR—or, for that matter, in Poland or South Africa—by diplomatic, economic or military pressure, it is hard to mount a convincing argument that absolute national invulnerability is a moral goal for Western nations to pursue. We need to give more attention to what it might mean to live in a world where all nations were to some extent committed to the risk of pressure, the possibility of change in response to external forces as well as internal development. More importantly, we need to take seriously what it means to belong to an international forum, the United Nations (UN), in which even the most powerful nation is open to censure. And beyond that lies the discovery of our need for 'common security', the recognition that there is no moral or practical sense in which a nation or group of nations can purchase total security for itself in isolation. The nuclear situation renders us all vulnerable; even the most optimistic advocate of Strategic Defence Initiative (SDI) has yet to come up with a plan that would decisively put one side for ever beyond risk—and that is as it should be.

The British Foreign Secretary said at Vienna in November 1986 that a climate of trust depends largely on a confidence that the same standards of behaviour and concepts of human welfare apply in the different countries engaged in negotiating arms reduction. It depends also on a recognition of common insecurity, a resolute turning away from policies that pursue security in isolation, and an acceptance of the necessary risks of political life in an uncertain world. The pursuit of common security alone delivers us from an idolatry of state security and sovereignty.

2. The Church and Loyalty

THE EARLY CHURCH

Where, then, should the Church stand in these matters of loyalty, legitimacy and sovereignty? The Church has its beginnings as a community standing in a complex and awkward relationship to the surrounding society, Jewish and pagan. Early Christian literature, inside and outside the New Testament, abounds in descriptions of believers as 'exiles' or resident aliens, people whose 'citizenship is in heaven'. The community—variously described in terms of 'people', 'kindred', 'city'—to which Christians belong cuts across the natural familial and social 'belonging' out of which they come. While the early Churches were not actively subversive of the social order, they were certainly seen as such. It was assumed that loyalty to the community was incompatible with family and political loyalties as understood in the Jewish and pagan environment of the day. Certainly the Church challenged the quasi-religious claims of kindred and state, and Christians, as is well-known, were executed for their refusal to take part in the cultus that sustained the identity of the Roman Empire. However, Christians were, at the same time, eager to claim continuity with Judaism on the one hand and to offer a kind of minimum practical loyalty to the Roman administration on the other. The Scillitan martyrs in the second century insisted that they paid taxes; apologists like Tertullian pointed out that Christians prayed for the rulers of the state and contributed to its survival and welfare by their standards of honesty and responsibility.

Christian reluctance to take part in the enforcement of law or the defence of the Empire continued to cause suspicion and hostility, but the Church could reasonably claim a constructive contribution to social life. Its loyalty to the state was, in fact, a very reduced version of the aforementioned third option—a belief in the goodness of order—without any very strong commitment to its maintenance, which could be seen to by others. Its primary loyalty was to a specific vision of human community in Christ; and despite some fourth-century attempts to fuse this loyalty with loyalty to a now nominally Christian empire, this identification never became normative. Augustine was to give classical expression to the distinction between the believer's commitment to the city of God and the detached, not unfriendly, but not passionate, concern such a person might feel for the survival of some kind of ordering of social relations in society at large. There are *relatively* just or partially just reasons for armed conflict or armed resistance, but no state is to be defended as having unconditional *justitia*. If it had, it would be the city of God itself, and the city of God cannot be defended by any earthly action, and *needs* no such defence, being rooted in God's eternal law. Thus states are always vulnerable, and never to be defended as if eternal verities depended on their survival.

THE REFORMATION

The Reformation did something to revive the ghost of an identification between the claims of the social order and the claims of the divine commonwealth. The godly prince was the defender of pure religion against papal absolutism; the freedom of the local church was guaranteed by the sovereign independence of the state. On the continent of Europe, the Wars of Religion were fuelled by these concerns. In Britain, the confirmation of royal control in the affairs of the Church, with the monarch as the final court of appeal, identified religious dissidence with crime (treason in extreme cases), and civil sedition with sacrilege. It is easy now to make light of what looks to the modern observer like a crudely ideological tactic; but in the context of the Reformation, it appeared obvious that papal sovereignty could be challenged only by national sovereignty ('this Realm of England is an Empire'), and that, given the assumption of a Christian people, whose souls were at stake, the Christian prince was entitled to legislate for his fellow-members in the body of Christ.

But the Reformation protest against papal monarchy held the seeds of a wider protest against control of the congregation's liberty by a prince who had no particular authority qua member of the body of Christ. Early Christian paradigms were revived, and the model of minimal 'secular' loyalty to a state making religious claims surfaced again, though it was no more persuasive to English than to Roman magistrates. It took nearly three centuries for English law fully to accommodate the reality of plural Christian allegiance within a single secular loyalty, and for dissenters, Catholic and Protestant, to be accepted as full citizens. The disestablishment of the Irish and Welsh Churches represented a final and radical concession to the principle of secular loyalty in a religiously plural state.

THE CHURCH OF ENGLAND

With such a history, however, it is not all that surprising if the Church of England has had difficulty in developing a theory and practice of critical detachment from the interests of the state; and the state in turn has reacted sharply in recent years to the Church's perceived refusal to assume that it is not to question the state's conduct of affairs or definition of its citizens' welfare. It is (whether we like it or not) a fact that the Church of England *belongs* in English society in ways that are still significant. But its own experience of marginality and powerlessness in many areas, as well as its recognition of the rapid and constant growth of religious diversity in the UK (not least the impressively large presence of Islam in some communities), has made it rightly more cautious about taking this 'belonging' for granted or being unduly swayed by appeals to it from those who resist what they see as negative and divisive social comment from the Church's representatives. A good many Anglicans today would, it appears, think of their primary political loyalty as being to a vision of the human community, to the struggle for justice and peace across the boundaries of nation-states; they are sceptical or openly critical of traditional patriotism, and generally reluctant to allow any religious seriousness to the claim of the state upon our commitment. The virtual identification of Anglican Christianity with 'Englishness' and of civic with religious loyalty had been under strain for so long that it was predictable that the reaction would be sharp. The unreality of this identification in ever larger tracts of English society, and the fact that Anglicanism was developing rapidly in post-colonial countries (not all of them even Anglophone) made the classical fusion of loyalties look, at best, like a sentimental muddle, and, at worst, a repressive fiction.

So it is no accident that the recent Inter-Anglican Theological and Doctrinal Commission report *(For the Sake of the Kingdom)* should put at the centre of its deliberations the problem of the Church's relation to culture which it helps to shape and which shapes it in turn, and also the culture where it appears a strange, foreign importation and must learn new habits of speech and action. The Christian Church, the report suggests, is constantly in a state of both belonging and not-belonging. Churches 'are at once natives of their places and foreigners in it, at once lovers and affirmers of its life and critics of its ways' (p.17 of the report). The 'both-and' here is important; in our reaction against easy identifications of secular with religious loyalty, we can forget that the universal struggle for a witness to the Kingdom only occurs among specific persons in particular contexts, with different languages and histories. Unless the Church is committed to making those languages and histories into vehicles and resources for proclaiming the Kingdom, what it says remains abstract. The local, the national, must be affirmed so that preaching and witness occur in the real world of men and women: the divine commonwealth does not occupy a neutral territory of its own where men and women live without their social constraints and historical limitations. If barriers are broken down in the Church, this need not mean that identities are reduced to a bare unhistorical minimum, or that the life of the Church stands in total discontinuity with the society in which it finds itself—even when its relation to that society is critical in some respects.

This holds even for the most radically separatist or 'sectarian' bodies, none of which have ever succeeded in creating a wholly self-enclosed culture expressing only Christian norms (even the Amish Mennonites reflect in large part a particular local and national ethos, that of Germany a century and a half ago). It is emphatically true for all the larger historic churches, Catholic, Protestant and Orthodox, and it suggests that *in practice* a loyalty to the Kingdom combined with a detached and general endorsement of the goodness of order without taking on the colouring of any specific environment is simply not a live option. We are always more involved than that. Even the great statement of the theology of social 'distance' in Augustine's *City of God* is also, paradoxically, a celebration of many elements in Roman civilisation. Augustine's point is that unless such elements are rightly related to the love of God, they become corrupt and destructive. This is the inevitable tragedy of purely secular politics. We need therefore to look at how we theologise about patriotism and 'national values' on the assumption that, while a bland religious endorsement of these things in their most unreconstructed form will not do, they need not be written off as no more than signs of fallenness or pride. They are not to be abandoned to secular ideology-making any more than to irrationalism and uncritical particularism.

3. Loyalty, Criticism and Hope

Raymond Williams defines a number of ways in which people may be said to 'belong' to their society, ranging from the passivity of a 'subject' to the full participation of a 'member'.[1] The 'member' has a share in determining and executing priorities; and we can assume that the particular quality of democratic society is that it expects and is meant to sustain *this* kind of belonging. And if there is to be a loyalty that is more than unreflective defensive emotion, it will be the loyalty of a 'member'—i.e. a commitment that is not to be separated from active involvement. This will be a loyalty that is not a blank cheque in the hands of rulers, licensing them to make unlimited and irresistible claims, but will be a faithfulness to a *process* in which the citizen has a role. I can make such a commitment out of the trust that this specific piece of human history, the language and conventions and system that have shaped where I stand, is not irredeemable, but has in it points containing the seeds of fruitful change. I affirm my context in the sense that I can engage with it in a significant way so as to further *here* the general human future I hope for. This is a context that, for all its ambiguities, can 'carry' some of the wider values to which I am committed.

But of course, I am not a member of British society in the way I might be of a Church or a political party. I do not *choose* to belong; as a rule, my membership is constituted by the accident of birth (not universally, insofar as there are people who decide for particular reasons to live in a context where they were not born;

but even here they are in some degree defined already by what they have inherited in the society they have left—think of the Soviet Jew in Israel). Like the family I belong to or the language I speak, my belonging to this or that political unit and social or legal framework is a matter beyond my control. And, as with family and language, nationality forms and conditions me in all sorts of ways—conscious and unconscious, obvious and not-so-obvious. I am, as an individual, *dependent* upon my context for my identity in all sorts of ways. But this clearly does not imply that I am always only passive in relation to these conditioning elements. My family relationships may or may not grow into adult human bonds, I may or may not find a truthful voice of my own as I learn to speak my language. I do not choose to belong to my context, but I can respond to it in a more or less creative way; I can *make* it my own in an adult sense. So my identity as an individual is never something I have the resource to make up out of my head; nor should it be something that is determined for me in advance by my surroundings. I form it within a 'conversation' and sometimes a struggle with history and language and cultural limits, and in so doing I do something to those limits. They help to form me; but, in however small a measure, I am changing and reshaping them as well.

The very idea of a *participatory* society is the way in which such considerations are translated into the terms of political practice. If the limits of language and kinship can be transformed as we interrelate with them, listening, responding and modifying what we receive, the same can be true of the social system and the political unit to which we belong. 'We cannot simply shed our nationhood,' says Keith Clements in his important study, *A Patriotism for Today: Dialogue with Dietrich Bonhoeffer* (p.118).[2] We begin by accepting where we stand, the bonds linking us to people and events, past and present, that we have not chosen; but to accept blindly and to defend blindly what is given is not a particularly human response. The question is, 'Out of this heritage, how shall we act so as to realise our own distinctive hopes?' Under what circumstances is what we are committed to really our own, something for which we are now prepared to take responsibility?

The Christian perspective can, perhaps, emphasise three things here. First it will remind us, by directing us to the worship of our maker, that there is no way out of our creatureliness, and so no way out of working with limits and identities we have not ourselves fully made or freely chosen. Secondly it will set before us a vision and a direction for what we are to make of what is given; and, as we have already noted, it will teach us about the nature of the final human horizon which is God's Kingdom, as it has already become real in the life and death and resurrection of Jesus. We are to ask not just 'What are we to make of this heritage?' but 'How are we to interact with this heritage so as to uncover and set free a *Christlike* humanity in ourselves and our children?' Thirdly, as Clements eloquently illustrates from the witness of Bonhoeffer, the Christian tradition, by urging us to, and enabling us for, truthfulness about our failures, will teach us to accept the *guilt* of our history and national identity (see especially pp. 104–109 of Clements' book). We shall 'make' nothing of our heritage unless we can see something of its darkness and ambivalence, of how people can be trapped by their history. To point to this need not be destructive—indeed, it is far more destructive to deny it or ignore it. Christian love is not blind. Christian love of nation, acceptance of it and commitment to it, can never rest on some sanitised, mythologised version of the state's past glories. It will celebrate real achievement and repent over real evil. It will remember that God's love is both merciful and truthful: it looks on sin with pity, and the very depth of that pity calls us to judgement and penitence. That is the love Christians seek to share in their relations to each other, and to the context in which they stand.

This suggests that Christian loyalty is a commitment to a nation conceived as being itself a process—of sharing, struggling and change; a commitment to what might be rather than simply what has been, though any such commitment to possible futures rests upon a sense of the past also, without which the future perspective becomes Utopian and abstract. Loyalty is the decision to be actively part of such a process. It therefore invites both criticism and hope—truthfulness about what it is in past and present that locks this process into destructive or unjust patterns, openness to an authoritative vision of what human community as such is in the purposes of God. In the last chapter it was argued that Christian hope is rooted in something that happens now, in lives being transformed by the Holy Spirit. This transformation affects not only isolated individuals but communities. If patriotism is seen in terms of commitment to a process of change in which we all have a role, then change for the better, the transformation that takes place as part of the process, will be seen by the Christian as, no less, the work of the Holy Spirit. Similarly, looking ahead to forthcoming chapters which discuss the possibilities for change now being revealed in international relationships, these too should be seen as intimately linked to patriotism, as understood here. For we have, not only in our own culture and in that of the cultures to which we relate, the seeds of fruitful change towards human community as it is meant to be. Russians are amongst the most patriotic people on earth but their true country, like ours, lies in the future. Loyalty is the belief that our situation and heritage has the resource to bring that vision to light, by the grace and mercy of God, in a distinct and fruitful way. It is, for the Christian, ultimately based on the loyalty of God to a human race that he refuses to abandon, whose limitations and sins do not defeat him. No person, no group, no nation, is wholly without the roots of promise and hope, because God is faithful to us in and through all our particularities—including our failures.

Conclusion

Keith Clements writes (op. cit. pp.52–53):

> In a world in which the issues of population, poverty, ecology and nuclear weaponry are inescapably everyone's issues, it has to be asked if, in Bonhoeffer's terms, the sovereign nation-state left to itself can even be an 'order of preservation'. Unless it is significantly qualified by a realistic world-consciousness, national identity seems destined to become an order of destruction rather than an order of preservation.

We might add that it is, of course, not only a matter of 'world *consciousness*' but the imperative of concrete co-operation in pursuit of shared human goals. Yet, as he goes on to say, the nation-state can claim a loyalty and love proper to it, precisely in its provisionality. The Christian can—and should—be committed to the state out of a trust that *this* history, *this* culture can manifest the promise of the Kingdom in its own uniquely enriching way. This commitment is expressed in creative engagement, active sharing in this community's life, and can be expressed too in a willingness to defend the community against those forces that seek to reduce or deny aspects of its multiform past and present—by open attack from outside, by totalitarian tendencies within. But as the individual seeks to share in a process of collaborative change and development, so, naturally, the ideal relation between different national/political communities is also one of involvement, challenge and collaboration. There is a way of defending one's heritage for its own sake, irrespective of its place in the whole project of the human race, or its witness to more than local values, that systematically undermines the possibility of constructive and critical exchange between societies. But that is to deny the whole basis of a properly Christian patriotism, a patriotism that is genuinely *human* in its horizons.

Hence the pertinence of this discussion to the nuclear problem. Clements remarks (p.122) that 'There can be no nuclear patriotism'; and if the account of patriotism developed in these pages is correct then the linking of nuclear hawkishness to patriotic seriousness is a mistake. It is possible to be patriotic, to be committed to one's place and people, without imagining that this must involve the quest for a total and exclusive security based on a massive and expanding nuclear arsenal. For the Christian, indeed, this is the only possibility, since the Christian above all is bound to search for a security that can be shared, and that rests on something more durably humane than total and permanent threat. There are some who argue that the maintenance of a minimum deterrent, combined with the active pursuit of arms reductions, is an unhappy necessity for the foreseeable future; but such people will recognise the danger in tying armaments to national pride and to the fantasy quest for final invulnerability. There are others who will argue that the mere possession of a nuclear arsenal entails the wrong kind of loyalty to country. But on both sides of this divide there can be agreement that there is a Christian case for commitment to and defence of the state in certain conditions, *and* an agreement about the dangers of mindless and uncritical loyalty, especially to a state whose obsession with security gradually destroys what it seeks to defend, and reproduces the very tyranny it fears. The common ground on which such Christian commentators may meet is, finally, that of the shared loyalty implicit in a shared baptism, being pledged to the vision of the Kingdom and to the God who has shown himself loyal to the world. This is never, though, loyalty to a purely abstract or ideal humanity; it is learned in the particular communities we cannot help belonging to, communities rightly loved, but loved for the sake of a greater community.

In one of the most nuanced reflections on patriotism in the English language, T. S. Eliot wrote:

> Love of a country
> Begins as attachment to our own field of action
> And comes to find that action of little importance
> Though never indifferent.
> History may be servitude, History may be freedom.
> See, now they vanish,
> The faces and places, with the self which, as it could, loved them,
> To become renewed, transfigured, in another pattern.
>
> (*Little Gidding* III)[3]

Without that 'pattern', and without the provisionality and critical distance implied, 'love of a country' is always in danger of degenerating into an unthinking corporate selfishness. Christian theology cannot afford to collude with that.

Summary

The Christian tradition maintains a careful and important balance between, on the one hand, a proper recognition of the state and of the people's membership of and loyalty to the national communities to which they belong, and, on the other hand, a steadfast refusal to absolutise the sovereignty of the state or the extent of the loyalty of individuals to it. States are always in a process of change. Christians are committed to this process in the direction of the Kingdom. The balance between states as they are and as they could be affects our view of the relationships between nations and states and, in the present discussion, the way we understand the claims of human rights in the contemporary task of establishing peaceful international relationships in our world (see Chapter 5). It further enables us to be ready to change in the character of the international order and of the relationships of states one to another. This will help us in facing up to the challenge of managing these changes and relationships for the purposes of peace in our world.

Footnotes

1 *The Long Revolution*, Raymond Williams. London, 1961.

2 *A Patriotism for Today: Dialogue with Dietrich Bonhoeffer*. Bristol Baptist College, 1984.

3 *Little Gidding* III, 159–165. T. S. Eliot.

4
East-West Perceptions

The Christian hope of peace reflects a vision of what the future could be but it is also rooted in the truth of the present, however bleak. As Chapter 2 discussed, Christians can have no truck with Utopianism. We have to begin with where we are, in the actual cultures in which we find ourselves. We will look at Europe in the context of the superpowers and then, with that background in mind, proceed to examine the way perceptions in East and West developed in the period after 1945 and how they stand today.

Europe and the Superpowers

The framework of British policy today is set by the existence of the two superpowers, the United States and the Soviet Union: deeply antagonistic, but each derived from a certain European tradition. This means that Europe should be a bridge between them as well as a battle ground. East Europeans can see virtues in the American system to which their Russian allies are blind. West Europeans often have insight into Soviet problems which their American associates do not share. Nonetheless, to regard Europe as being equidistant and 'non-aligned' between the superpowers would be a false deduction from the history of their relationship and it is necessary to demonstrate why this is so.

Unlike the Soviet Union, the United States was very largely settled by European immigrants who took their own cultural patterns with them. (This is, of course, to ignore the significant exception of forcible African immigration, which might, had the Civil War not been fought, have created a very different type of American society.) Not least important were their religious observances. If the United States was constituted as a secular society, it was because of the intensity and diversity of the religious beliefs held by the American colonists, not their absence. These beliefs survive with a far greater vigour than they do in Europe, and any committed Christian visiting the United States can only be envious of the flourishing state of the Churches throughout the community; even though he may be bewildered or even repelled by the form which many of their observances take. The United States is a Christian community, or rather a multiplicity of Christian communities which provides Christians in Europe with the opportunity for something more than an inter-state dialogue as well as a deep root of common concern.

The public philosophy of the United States, however, is not religious but explicitly secular. It is the philosophy, which has remained almost unsullied over 200 years, of the eighteenth century Enlightenment. It proclaims the perfectibility of 'man' by individual effort, responsibility for his own destiny, and an innate right to work out his own secular and transcendental salvation in his own way so long as he does not trespass on the rights of others. Founded on a belief in the supremacy of reason, it was seen at the time as profoundly liberating, as indeed it was. Its effects are still working themselves out throughout the world. Marxists dismiss this creed as the ideological superstructure of capitalism; non-Marxists see the development of free enterprise economy as being at least as much the effect of this doctrine as its cause. Whichever analysis is correct, however, belief in 'free enterprise' (as its friends call it) or 'capitalism' (as its critics prefer) remains a fundamental article of American faith: one so universal and so pervasive that all attempts to build up a serious socialist party in the United States have failed. To be sure, there has developed over the past 50 years an enormous public sector of the economy which Republican administrations do their best to cut back; while the private sector has fallen largely into the hands of a number of gigantic corporations who control the economy between them. But the ideology and the rhetoric remains unchanged and retains its power to evoke deep and widespread commitment throughout all classes of American society.

As this belief grew in nineteenth-century America—fuelled by the opening of the territories in the West, strengthened by the defeat of the slavocracy in the Southern States—so in Europe it came under attack. Its embodiment in revolutionary France associated it with emerging and mutually hostile national movements, which rejected both the universalism of the Enlightenment and its emphasis on the individual. Nations grow from their own cultural roots and their culture moulds the individual: so argued Herder and the school of nationalists who followed him. So the state—the instrument of the nation—must have primacy; a view reinforced by the growing concern in Europe over the appalling social conditions produced by the unrestrained private enterprise of the early industrial era. It was a concept adopted by Marxists, who substituted for the idea of *nation* that of *class*. By the end of the century, all the advanced industrial states of Europe had developed various degrees of *etatisme* designed to forestall the revolution depicted by Marx, which on the whole they successfully did. In some parts of Europe, the emphasis on community was not originally associated with *etatisme*. In Britain, Scandinavia, or the Low Countries, it was rather the consequence of the formation of independent associations, trade unions or co-operatives or non-conformist Churches, which could afford the individual some protection both from the economic privations caused by industrialisation and from the authoritarianism of the state. It may well have been the existence of this non-statist notion of community that allowed for more democratic peaceful forms of change in these countries.

This emphasis on collectivism set them all, to a greater or lesser degree, on a course divergent from that of the United States. Taken to extreme, it led to the totalitarian and the nationalistic excesses of fascism; a creed hostile equally to capitalist free enterprise and to international socialism, drawing its strength from deep irrational and counter-rational forces released by the collapse of the European order in the first two decades of this century. The defeat of Nazi Germany and her sympathisers cleared the air. The forces of the Right in Europe had to accept the liberal ideological framework imposed by their American rescuers, though malodorous pools of feudal nostalgia or nationalist obstinacy remained to complicate the transatlantic relationship. The forces of the Left, on the whole, accepted that framework as well: the behaviour of the Soviet Union in the years immediately after the war left them with little choice (although most countries were able to carry out Social Democratic programmes).

The Russian experience has been profoundly different from that of the West European, and even more from the American. Russian culture derives from Byzantium rather than from Rome and from the beginning Russian nationalists sharply differentiated their tradition from those of the West. That tradition was one of highly authoritarian government by a Czar who was God's anointed and father to his people, his authority sanctified by a purely supportive and apolitical Church. This authoritarianism was indigenous, concepts of democracy (above a basic village commune level) exogenous. The scientific and technological revolutions of the seventeenth century and the 'Englightenment' of the eighteenth were imported from the West by a succession of 'Westernising' Czars and their advisers, from Peter the Great onward, to enable them to compete on the European stage with their Western neighbours. By the beginning of the twentieth century there had developed in Russia a sophisticated Westernised élite which represented Russia in the international community, but their numbers were tiny and the gulf between them and the peasant masses remained enormous. (The similarity with the situation in many 'Third World' nations today is striking.) When the structure of Czarist authoritarianism collapsed in 1917 under the strain of war, there was no effective governing class ready to take over and run the country on Western lines. The only group strong enough to prevail in the ensuing chaos was the communist faction led by Lenin and later Stalin, which turned its back on Western concepts of socialism, based its power on the peasant masses and ruled with all the ruthless authoritarianism of the Czars.

In spite of the purge of the 'Westernising' old Bolsheviks and the murder of Trotsky, the degree to which the Soviet Union had turned its back on Western ideas of socialism and democracy was not at first generally appreciated by Western intellectuals desperately anxious to see the socialist experiment succeed. The fortuitous alliance between Stalin and the Western democracies in the

Second World War provided further incentive for glossing over the more unacceptable elements in the beliefs and practices of so necessary an ally. But the harshness with which Stalin rejected the West after the war and the ruthlessness with which he eliminated diversity—especially communist diversity—in the European territories conquered or reconquered by Soviet armies made it clear that Soviet society was now guided by alien values of a kind which made dialogue with the West almost impossible. Expectations of Soviet aggression against the West were almost certainly exaggerated, but pessimism about the possibility of any serious co-operation over the peaceful settlement of Europe was not. A *modus vivendi* was established on the minimalist basis of *cuius regio, eius religio*: the political configuration of Europe was determined by lines drawn, and defended, by military power, and has remained so ever since. All but a tiny minority of socialists, and all 'bourgeois democrats' came to accept if they had to live under the aegis of one of the superpowers that their values would survive better in a region dominated by the United States than one controlled by the Soviet Union.

The United States and the Soviet Union differ from the states of Europe in that they define themselves not so much in terms of history and nationality as of ideology. They are both 'dedicated to propositions' which form the basis of their entire educational systems. Neither has much sympathy with or understanding of societies whose history has bred different social and political concepts. This makes for American impatience with the complexities of Europe and European impatience with the 'naivety' of America. Nevertheless, intrinsic to the American system is the acceptance of diversity. The platitudes of its public policy veil the almost infinite complexities of a deeply libertarian society. American policies and attitudes are constantly being questioned by Americans. There is no topic of dialogue between Europeans and Americans which is not also one of dialogue—usually at a far deeper level of passion and expertise—among Americans themselves. European voices are welcomed in the United States and listened to attentively, if sometimes with bewilderment. There is certainly disagreement and often dislike, but fundamentally our cultural values remain the same—if only acceptance of the right of free speech and the rule of law. Where there is abrogation of these in associated countries, it is American voices that are loudest in condemnation.

The problem about the Soviet Union is its *suppression* of diversity; not only for its own people but those under its control. The Church is indeed tolerated, but only on condition that it abstains totally from political involvement—a prohibition which the Poles never have accepted and never will. We are only now beginning to emerge from the decades during which dialogue at any level, or on any topic, elicited only a repetition of approved official orthodoxies, authenticated by reference to the sacred texts of Lenin and a heavily-expurgated Marx. The diversity of Western culture is seen as bewildering by the Russian people and threatening by their leaders. The latter are in exactly the same position as their predecessors, Peter and Catherine the Great: they need the science and technology of the West to increase the power and wealth of the state, they may privately flirt with Western ideas, but they see Western culture in its totality as being profoundly subversive of the entire system, and they go often to absurd lengths to protect their people from it. Under Gorbachev, this may be changing. Gorbachev's own speeches and writings seem to suggest a longing to rejoin the Western world and to end the pariah status of the Soviet Union.

The problem we face at present is how to develop the dialogue which has already begun with a society whose means of communication are so rigorously controlled. Were such a dialogue to develop, based on equal access to a common fund of information, then the nature of Europe's historical experience and the insights it can provide into Soviet problems and perceptions might make it more possible for us to act as a bridge across the East-West divide instead of the battlefield we constitute at present.

Legacy of the Second World War

Loyalty and commitment to a country, which were discussed in Chapter 3, have since ancient times been regarded as implying a readiness to rally to its defence when it is under threat. In the course of the 43-year history of the nuclear age, that threat has come to assume dimensions which would have been unimaginable to anyone who was not living when nuclear weapons were first used at Hiroshima and Nagasaki. Fear and suspicion have led to an arms race which has continued for four decades. Even now, as there are fresh hopes that ways may be found to slow down the accumulation of weapons and even to make significant reductions, the arms race is still a phenomenon which seems to have acquired a self-perpetuating energy of its own.

An arms race, however, does not occur between countries which enjoy a stable relationship of mutual confidence: it is set in motion by fear and suspicion on the part of one nation or group of nations about the motives and ambitions of another and by concern about the military, economic and political threat which it is seen as presenting. It is a matter of the way each side sees the other; a matter of perceptions, truthful or misleading, and intentions, which may be assessed with accuracy or misinterpreted.

Shared language and culture make it easy for one country to understand the aims and policies of another; the US and Canada do not have serious difficulties arising from their perceptions of each other. Linguistic and cultural differences can sometimes cause friction even between countries closely linked by alliance, partnership and friendship, such as Britain and France; but it is a task of diplomacy to reconcile the differences. Between the states of Western Europe and North America on the one hand and the Soviet Union on the other, as we have seen the differences are many and varied. When we come to consider détente and reconciliation in Chapter 9 we will need to consider differences of ideology, political culture and national power.

The origins of the Cold War have been widely discussed, and sharply differing interpretations have been put on wartime and postwar events by historians in the East and in the West, and indeed by various groups of historians in the West. One group places responsibility for the conflict upon the Soviet Union; it argues that the United States and Britain saw Soviet domination of Eastern Europe as a threat to their hopes of a postwar settlement in Europe based on co-operation and on democratic principles. But adherents of this view differ in their explanations of America's seemingly passive attitude to this expansion of

Soviet influence. Some argue that at the time there was little understanding in Washington of the significance of Soviet actions in Eastern Europe, others that the United States was well aware of what was happening but lacked the means or the will to react effectively. Another group of historians, often known as revisionists, place responsibility for the conflict on the United States, arguing that the United States used the spectre of a Soviet invasion of Western Europe in order to keep Western Europe within the US sphere of influence. On this view, the US as well as the establishments in Western European countries were thus enabled to create what amounted to an Atlantic free trade area and to thwart the aspirations of socialist and communist political forces in Western Europe. According to this interpretation, Western rearmament and the attachment of unacceptable conditions to the offer of Marshall Aid to Eastern Europe strengthened Stalin's determination to tighten his grip on Eastern Europe.

The origins of the wartime disagreement over policy towards the states of Eastern Europe, however, and consequently the wider dispute which led to the creation of NATO and the Warsaw Pact are probably to be found in the differing Anglo-American and Soviet interpretations of the Atlantic Charter. This declaration of principles, agreed upon by President Roosevelt and Winston Churchill on 14th August 1941, required that there should be no territorial changes that did not accord with the freely expressed wish of the peoples concerned and that all peoples had the right to choose the form of government under which they would live. These principles were approved in September 1941 by all governments then at war with Germany, and after the entrance of the US into the war, all the allied governments pledged themselves to fulfil them. The establishment of Communist systems of government in the countries of Eastern Europe in the wake of the victorious Soviet advance was seen by the United States Government as a clear breach of these principles. The Atlantic Charter principles represented the tradition of Woodrow Wilson, the tradition of dislike and suspicion for 'spheres of influence' and secret deals about the destinies of peoples. It was hardly to be expected that, with its wholly different traditions, the Soviet

Union would interpret them in the same spirit. The conclusion reached by Lynn Davis from her study of the origins of the Cold War brings out this basic misconception:

> . . . the ideas held by American officials about how peace should be constructed after the war—an end to balance-of-power diplomacy and the creation of representative governments—precluded United States acceptance of a Soviet sphere of influence in Eastern Europe or willingness to live in a divided Europe in 1945. They could not approve Soviet efforts to establish predominant political influence in this part of the world through the imposition of minority Communist regimes. Consequently, as early as 1942 Soviet unilateral policies in Eastern Europe provoked perceptions of rising Soviet aggressiveness.[1]

On the Soviet side, whatever other ambitions may have existed, there was determination that the states of Eastern Europe should never again be the avenue through which aggression could reach Soviet territory. The opening of the nuclear age in 1945 gave the United States a monopoly—for a few years—of the most destructive weapon on earth. Exhausted after its long struggle and heavy human losses, the Soviet Union was plainly concerned to maximise the fruits of victory and to make the needs of its own security paramount. The concept of common European security, which had proved illusory for the Soviet Union in 1939, would have few attractions until, years later, the vast build-up of nuclear weapons made clear that nuclear war could never be a sensible way to pursue the aims of national policy.

The aims of Soviet policy at this time were not always easy to understand from the public speeches of Stalin and other leaders. Apart from their length and their jargon-laden character, they were often expressed in the arcane terminology of Marx-Leninism. According to this interpretation there was a sharp division between the forces of 'peace and progress' headed by the Soviet Union, and the forces of reaction which were ranged in fierce, but in the long run futile, opposition to them. As the laws of the development of human societies and the unfolding of history, as described in the teachings of Marx and Lenin, forecast the victory of the forces of peace and progress and made it a matter of duty for Communists to facilitate that victory, the inference was drawn by Western opponents that the Soviet Union, however carefully its aims were disguised in ideological trappings, was set on an expansionist course. Large Soviet forces remained undemobilised; Soviet diplomacy did not seem interested in reaching agreements; and the Soviet press was writing in unfriendly terms about the policies and the leaders of the nations which a few years earlier had been the allies of the Soviet Union. Many people in the West were puzzled at the conduct of a nation which had only recently been a comrade in arms in the defeat of Fascism and Nazism.

From the personal memoirs of statesmen and from official documents released in Western countries, a mass of information is now available to show how, at the time of the formation of NATO, Western leaders perceived the Soviet Union and its aims. The *coup d'état* which secured for the Communists the complete control of Czechoslovakia in February 1948 and the blocking by the Soviet Union of surface traffic from the West to Berlin in a few months later, resulting in the Berlin airlift, were seen in Western capitals as worrying evidence of Soviet intentions. There was also concern at this time that the large Communist Parties in France and Italy would be victorious in the elections and would form governments or play a major role in them. A shared sense of alarm led rapidly to the signature of the North Atlantic Treaty and the formation of NATO. This dramatic step was intended as a diplomatic signal that the nations of the West would act to stop armed aggression. How this Western move was perceived in Moscow is still a matter of speculation but it is virtually certain that the Russian leaders did not see it solely for what it was—as evidence of the will of democracies to defend themselves. George Kennan, whose years of experience in Moscow before and during the Second World War qualified him to judge how the Russians would view the Western action, sent this analysis to Washington in 1952 while serving as US Ambassador in Moscow:

> The Kremlin leaders were attempting in every possible way to weaken and destroy the structure of non-Communist world. In the course of this endeavour they were up to many things which gave plenty of cause of complaint on the part of Western statesmen. They would not have been surprised if these things had been made the touchstone of Western reaction. But why, they might ask, were they being accused

> precisely of one thing they had *not* done which was to plan, as yet, to conduct an overt and unprovoked invasion of Western Europe? Why was the imputation to them of this intention being put forward as the rationale for Western re-armament? Did this not imply some ulterior purpose . . .?[2]

The United States emerged from the Second World War with its industrial strength unimpaired; over large areas of the Soviet Union industry and agriculture had been devastated by the 'scorched earth' policy and by the passage of armies, and the population of the Soviet Union had been, in the literal sense of the word, decimated. Although its armed forces were reduced by rapid demobilisation, the United States must have appeared as a formidable adversary and one which had many advantages in the development and production of modern military equipment. Moreover, the positions held by the capitalist powers in the postwar world may well have seemed unassailable when viewed from the perspective of the Kremlin. From a Western perspective, the exhaustion of the Soviet Union after its bitter struggle with Germany seemed less significant than the large Soviet armies still deployed in Eastern Europe, the menacing tone of the speeches made by the Soviet leaders, and the uncompromising attitude of Soviet representatives in negotiations for a postwar settlement in Europe.

Had the Russians been less addicted to their own traditional practices of secrecy and to a preference for the use of clandestine methods, Western suspicions might have been less pronounced. On the Western side, the habit common to military planners of preparing for the worst case was encouraged by the more alarming estimates of Soviet military strength which were provided by intelligence agencies. These were the years in which, on each side, the 'military-industrial complex', whose existence was acknowledged by both Eisenhower and Krushchev, gained strength and influence. Mutual ignorance fed suspicion; suspicion in turn reinforced convictions on each side that the intentions of the other were devious, cloaked by hypocrisy and deeply malign. On each side an image was formed of an adversary whose intentions were menacing and hostile. In such situations it is usual that information which does not conform to the accepted image is ignored or disparaged, its validity is denied or its meaning twisted so that it seems to confirm, or at least not to contradict, the currently accepted belief. Corroborative evidence, by contrast, is quickly, accurately and eagerly noted. The stereotypes and images thus formed in the minds of many people can easily become self-reinforcing, durable and difficult to eradicate even when important changes occur in the world outside. Old habits of thought, like other habits, die hard.

The Last 40 Years

From the moment when the postwar confrontation between the Warsaw Pact and NATO assumed the pattern which, broadly speaking, has remained constant for over 35 years, the assessment of military capability of the adversary's fleets, armies and air forces and the gauging of the political intentions of the leaders of the nations of the opposed alliance have been the unending concern of East and West. The king in Luke 14.31 who, when going to encounter another king in war, sat down first and took counsel whether he was able with 10,000 men to meet him who came against him with 20,000 men was certainly not the first leader to be worried about the capability of his adversary and the nature of the military balance. The forces of the other side are menacing simply because one can be clear and certain about one's own peaceable intentions but it is never possible to obtain the same certainty about an adversary, especially one given to secretiveness and suspicion. Earl Grey of Fallodon, the British Foreign Secretary in 1914, wrote:

> The distinction between preparations made with the intention of going to war and precautions against attack is a true distinction, clear and definite in the minds of those who build up armaments. But it is a distinction that is not obvious and certain to others . . . Each Government, therefore, while resenting any suggestion that its own measures are anything more than defence, regards similar measures of another Government as preparation to attack.[3]

Earl Grey's remarks have lost little of their relevance in the nuclear age; but whereas mistakes in perception at an earlier time could result in defeat today they could result in annihilation.

Crude assessments of armed forces available to a potential adversary have given place to highly sophisticated and refined analyses made by each alliance of the naval, military and air capability of the opposing alliance and the strength and disposition of its nuclear forces in all categories. The confrontation of large armed forces in Europe has, through the passage of time, acquired a certain stability. Year by year confidence has increased in each alliance that it can divine more accurately than before the intentions of the other side. This uneasy situation has survived crises like those of 1956 (Hungary and Suez), 1962 (Cuban Missile Crisis), and 1973 (Arab-Israeli war) which made the outbreak of war seem perilously close. These crises, which are among the textbook cases of crisis management, taught each side much about the reactions of the other. So also did Soviet behaviour during the Vietnam war and Western behaviour during the Polish crisis in 1981. Navigating a way through these dangerous reefs provided each of the adversaries with convincing evidence that for the other there was no priority higher than the avoidance of nuclear war.

The decade of the seventies brought a welcome relaxation of East-West tension but détente unfortunately did not bring with it an end to East-West misunderstanding. The hopes encouraged by the signature of the Strategic Arms Limitation Treaty (SALT) and the Anti-Ballistic Missile Treaty of 1972 and the Helsinki Final Act of 1975 were welcome evidence that, with patient diplomacy, progress in reconciling East-West differences was possible. Even if the agreements themselves did not actually reduce the level of armaments on each side they reduced the tension and gave hope of further more substantial progress to come. The agreements themselves, however, were in part the cause of the misunderstandings that followed. The SALT agreement did not seem to the Russians to preclude the introduction of a new class of missiles which were of medium range and therefore were not strategic weapons; but the deployment of these missiles was seen in the West as calling for a response, which took the form of deployment of Cruise and Pershing II missiles. Such misunderstandings are by no means confined to the political and military spheres. They have hitherto been characteristic of the way in which the West and its society is looked upon by Russians.

Perceptions—True and False

Whatever the state of the military or political imbalance between East and West, there can be little doubt of the continuing advantage enjoyed by the advanced Western nations in the level of industrial technology. Yet this is a subject which reveals Russian attitudes of great complexity which have roots deep into Russian history. This is poignantly illustrated by the nineteenth-century story told by Nicolai Leskov. It tells of a clockwork flea so small that it could only be seen with a microscope, made by British craftsmen and bought by Czar Alexander I in London as proof of the superior skill of British craftsmen. The next Czar, determined that Russia should not be shown up as inferior, sought Russian craftsmen to match the skill of the British craftsmen. Four Russian smiths from Tula, with no special equipment, shod the flea with metal shoes. The Czar sent one of them to London to show the British 'what sort of craftsmen we have in Tula'. The story is familiar to all Russians and never far from their minds at moments of Soviet triumphs in space; not surprisingly a British minister was puzzled when Mr Gorbachev, on his London visit in 1984, remarked, 'If you send us a flea we will put horsehoes on it.'[4] The message would have been clear to a Russian. Gorbachev was not following Alexander I in his 'obeisance before things from abroad' (a favourite phrase of Stalin) but was boldly displaying the attitudes of Alexander I's successor; if the new contest with the West was on the technological front, the Russians would give as good as they got. Time alone will show whether economic change in Russia robs Leskov's story of its relevance or whether its picture of Russian complexes about the West will remain a recognisable one for some time to come.

The failures of Russian industry and agriculture, the drabness of Russian shops and the perennial shortages are a matter of constant comment in the Western Press and are always remarked on by visitors. But here too there is a distinct ambivalence in Russian attitudes to the values of the money-conscious societies of the West. The profusion of goods on sale in Western countries evokes a complex reaction in which moral superiority is as important as envy and more common than resentment. Ordinary

Russians balance eagerness to acquire Western goods with scornful comments such as 'In the West people will do anything for money.' A writer in *Komsomolskaya Pravda*, which aims at young readers, had this to say in 1983:

> The highest value in the West is money. Or its equivalent, goods. The most respected person in that society is the one who knows how to make money . . . Our highest value is the moral man, the harmoniously developed personality. The equality of people. Absolutely not money and not goods . . .[5]

Nevertheless, the attractions of Western consumerism remain powerful and the old notions of the austere moral rectitude of Russia in the face of the attractions offered by the seductive but morally bankrupt and historically doomed societies of the West are less and less persuasive to a new generation for whom Stalin, the 'Great Patriotic War' and even Khrushchev are no more than pages of history.

There is, to be sure, an immense difference between the levels of understanding among experts and among people at large. The huge resources devoted by Western governments, universities and institutes to the study and understanding of the Soviet Union, its organisation, its aims and policies and its attitudes to the West, mean the misperceptions and misunderstandings are less likely than in earlier decades. On the Soviet side, many of the experts whose duty it is to interpret developments in the West in the framework of Marx-Leninism have at least the advantage of many years experience of the West to reduce the risk of error. Nevertheless, errors can and do occur on both sides. The experience of the 1970s was an example. The West, relieved that tension had been relaxed by the 1972 Strategic Arms Limitation Treaty and the 1973 US-Soviet Agreement on the Avoidance of Nuclear War, paid insufficient attention to Soviet public pronouncements that 'the class struggle of the two systems in the sphere of economics, politics and, it goes without saying, ideology, will be continued . . . The world outlook and the aims of socialism and capitalism are opposed and irreconcilable.' Soviet involvement in Ethiopia and Angola and failure to fulfil the human rights obligations of the Helsinki Final Act created the impression in the West that the Soviet Union had failed to honour its bargains. Anti-Soviet sallies had long been a regular feature of American elections, but certain remarks by the President, like his reference to 'the aggressive impulses of an evil empire', accompanied by a sharp increase in US defence appropriations, led President Brezhnev to remark that the danger of war was greater than at any time since 1945. Dismissed at the time as propaganda hyperbole, this remark was, according to contemporary reports, stimulated by real Soviet anxiety that the West might genuinely be contemplating physical rather than merely verbal aggression. Once again, as with previous American and Soviet speeches, the speaker's confidence that the honourable and peaceful nature of his motives would be apparent to his adversaries was misplaced. Even after 40 postwar years of experience, misperception and misinterpretation are still fairly easy.

The ideas entertained by individuals in Western countries and in the Soviet Union about each other's societies are even more susceptible to errors sometimes of a ludicrous kind. As the incident recounted by Colin Thubron and quoted in the Preface of this report brings out, there are some strange misconceptions.[6] Such surprising misconceptions no doubt have their parallels in the West, despite the ready availability in Western countries of a mass of information about life in Eastern Europe. However, many aspects of life, from politics to pop music, are a subject of boundless and constant curiosity to hundreds and thousands, and the appetite for information has grown since controls to it have been relaxed. In the West, however careful the study of Eastern Europe by experts, public interest has tended to be fitful; it is stimulated by dramatic events such as the shooting down of the Korean airliner or the Chernobyl nuclear disaster. Since Mr Gorbachev began his series of major changes in every aspect of Soviet life, however, interest in Soviet affairs has risen sharply. There is more news to report about events in the Soviet Union and Eastern Europe; the revelation of past and current abuses and the open discussion of matters hitherto subject to censorship have brought Soviet affairs daily into the headlines in the West. This increase in interest in what the Soviet Union is really like will help to give more accuracy, subtlety and depth to the perception which the average person has of the Soviet Union.

The changes now going on in the Soviet Union are of profound significance, not merely for the Soviet Union itself, but for the future of East-West relations. There may now be signs of hope that this sad legacy of the years in which East-West contacts were resisted and discouraged by the Soviet Union may at long last be reduced and eventually made no more dangerous to peace than the misconceptions of the Caucasian farmer about the Queen and Mrs Thatcher (as quoted in the introduction).[6]

Television, radio and the press now play a powerful role in forming perceptions, for better or for worse. Their power was most vividly demonstrated at the time of the 1987 meeting between President Reagan and Mr Gorbachev in Washington and its successor in Moscow in June 1988. The 1987 meeting will be remembered for the image of the two leaders smiling during the ceremony at which they signed the treaty eliminating the entire class of intermediate and medium-image nuclear weapons. Amid the enormous media attention given to this event, the importance of perceptions was emphasised by *Time* magazine:

> In diplomacy, especially in the age of television, the perception that tensions have been reduced tends to mean that tensions have in fact been reduced. What happened in Washington last week is that the perceptions changed measurably—and for the better—on both sides.[7]

Summary

We have seen how Christian understandings of peace and hope commit us to work for their realisation in the present. We need, therefore, to understand the distinctive and sometimes conflicting histories and perceptions which we bring to the task of making peace. We need to see Europe in relation both to the United States and to the Soviet Union. We need also to seek to understand the issues as they are perceived in both the East and the West.

In this chapter we have sought to present the different perceptions of why we have our present divisions. A better understanding of why others see things as they do, however different such perceptions are to our own, is in itself an important step in the task of making peace. These provide the map from which we can plot a way for détente and even for reconciliation. These are matters which we will pursue in Chapter 9.

Footnotes

[1] *The Cold War Begins*, Lynn Davis. Princeton University Press, 1974, p.394.

[2] *Memoirs*, Vol. 2, 1950–63, George Kennan. Little, Brown (Boston), 1972, pp.335–6.

[3] *Twenty Five Years*, Lord Grey. Hodder & Stoughton, 1925. p.91.

[4] Leskov's story 'The Left-Handed Craftsman' was published in 1881. The story and the 1984 episode in London are recounted by Mark Frankland in *The Sixth Continent*. Hamish Hamilton, 1987, pp.264–5.

[5] Frankland, *op. cit.*, p.234.

[6] *Among the Russians*, Colin Thubron. Penguin Books, 1985, p.183.

[7] *Time*, 21st December 1987.

5
Human Rights and Arms Control

Shalom is not the absence of tension but the presence of justice. One essential aspect of this justice is the observance of basic human rights not only in one's own country but universally. For, as we argued in Chapter 3, the understanding of sovereignty in which every country is a law to itself and no country has a right to concern itself with the internal affairs of other countries, cannot be justified on theological grounds.

When, in 1876, Mr Gladstone denounced the treatment by the Ottoman Empire of its subjects in the territory which is today Bulgaria, he voiced a sense of outrage which was widely felt in Britain at the time. Violation of human rights in one country often causes concern, even anger and outrage, in another, and the strength of public feeling on this emotive question is no novelty in international relations. It was, however, only after the Second World War that the notion of human rights was enshrined in an international document endorsed by the whole community of independent nations. The Universal Declaration of Human Rights was adopted without opposition by the General Assembly of the United Nations in 1948, and thus the question of human rights, the violations of which by Nazi Germany and others in the preceding decade had shocked the conscience of world, secured a permament place on the agenda of international life.

It was not until the early 1970s that human rights became an active subject of dispute between East and West. In the early 1970s the opinion was voiced by many, most notably in the United States, that concessions to the Soviet Union on trade and on arms control and disarmament issues should be made conditional on better treatment by the Soviet Government of its own citizens. These demands centred on such issues as the granting of exit visas to individuals in the Soviet Union who wished to emigrate. Often these were people wishing to join members of their families who were already abroad, and from whom they had been separated by the withholding of permission to leave the country. There was also pressure for the release from prison or return from exile of those punished under Soviet law for 'anti-Soviet acts' of a kind which in Western societies would not be considered offences at all. To people in Western countries this seemed to be a denial of basic political rights, even though the Soviet authorities claimed that the punishments were in accordance with Soviet law. In addition, Western opinion was dismayed at reports that dissidents were being confined to psychiatric hospitals because they had expressed dissentient political opinions. 'Samizdat' publications emerging from the Soviet Union spread knowledge of the names of those being detained and the conditions of their detention. Pressure groups, particularly in the United States, were active in using this information to influence the policy of the government. The United States government, and to a lesser degree other Western governments, were thus faced with two questions; should human rights issues be allowed to affect the course of negotiations with the Soviet Union on arms control and disarmament issues? If such means were used to apply pressure to the Soviet Union, would the result be to change the way in which the Soviet government treated its citizens, or merely to exacerbate an already difficult relationship with the Soviet Union without achieving an improvement in the treatment of those citizens for whose benefit the pressures were applied?

That these questions should be raised at all was in terms of international law a surprising innovation. Broadly speaking the view of the positivist international lawyers of the eighteenth and nineteenth centuries was that states were the only subject of international law and that individuals could only be the objects of understandings between states. Thus the notion of human rights and duties as something belonging to individuals in their own right and not as subjects of states has, in the words of Hedley Bull,[1] become 'potentially subversive of international society itself'. The basic concept of coexistence between states, expressed in the exchange of recognition of sovereign jurisdictions, implies a conspiracy of silence entered into by governments about the rights and duties of their respective citizens. What one state chose to do to its own citizens was, on this theory, a matter for that state alone and no business of any other state. It was not, therefore, surprising that when President Theodore Roosevelt's administration protested to the government of Czar Nicholas II of Russia about the violation of human rights in Russia, the protest was curtly rejected on the grounds that the matter was one wholly within the Czar's jurisdiction. The doctrine that one state should not interfere in the internal affairs of another has frequently been used since then as the ground for rejection of complaints about human rights violations. The adoption of the Universal Declaration of Human Rights in 1948 marked an important change in this regard; but the Declaration could only be effectively invoked in respect of those states which had given their assent to it, and in any case the Declaration did not itself have the force of law. Moreover, the Soviet Union abstained on the vote on the Declaration rather than endorsing it.

Whatever the purely legal considerations might be, there was undoubtedly a feeling in the United States in 1973 that American indignation over the fate of the Russian dissenters should be expressed openly and at the highest level to the Soviet government. Indeed Secretary Weinberger and Secretary Schultz, at that time members of President Nixon's cabinet, were criticised in the *New York Times* as being willing in the interests of trade and détente to shunt aside the concern of the American people for human rights everywhere.[2] This concern, encouraged by the continuing publicity given to the plight of the dissidents in the Soviet Union, led to the inclusion of provisions relating to human rights in the so-called 'Third Basket' of the Final Act of the Conference of Security and Co-operation in Europe (CSCE), signed in Helsinki in 1975 and generally held to mark one of the most notable achievements of the East-West détente of the 1970s. In a juridical and political sense this was no exaggeration. For the first time, obligations in regard to human rights had become part of an international instrument which, although lacking the force of a formal treaty, was endorsed by 35 nations including the great powers of East and West. Thus, for the first time, there were certain agreed obligations and standards in regard to human rights. Each signatory of the Final Act was expected to lend its authority to ensuring that the standards were met in its territory.

It would have been difficult to think of an issue more certain to cause dissent between East and West, nor one which went closer to the heart of the dispute between the Western liberal democracies and the Marx-Leninist countries of Eastern Europe. It would, however, be wrong to suggest that the Soviet Union declined to recognise human rights. The Soviet Union certainly recognised human rights, but a wholly different hierarchy of rights. It gave prominence to group rights over those of individuals; it proclaimed the economic and social rights of peoples in preference to the civil and political rights of individuals. In the provision of economic and social rights it claimed superiority over the capitalist nations of the West. It boasted that the Soviet Union and the Peoples' Democracies of Eastern Europe surpassed the Western nations in giving their peoples the assurance of work and the right to enjoy the benefits of education and leisure irrespective of wealth or social status. Indeed, the Soviet Union in the 1950s went on the offensive, describing the Universal Declaration on Human Rights as inadequate and claiming that its adoption in 1948 had represented a triumph of the peoples over the forces of imperialism. The Soviet Diplomatic Dictionary of 1960 gave the following account of the Declaration:

> The adoption of the Universal Declaration of Human Rights reflected those world historical changes in international relations which are taking place as a result of the growth of the forces of democracy, peace and socialism. The imperialist countries were not in a position to ignore the unanimous demands of the peoples for defence of the rights of the individual and democracy.[3]

Whatever may have been the political motives of the Soviet Union in adopting this position, there could be little doubt that it was a natural consequence of the view adopted by Karl Marx of the bourgeois theory of natural rights expounded by Locke, Rousseau and other philosophers of the Enlightenment. Marx criticised their theories of natural rights as no more than special pleading by members of privileged economic class seeking to defend their own interests. The right of the individual to liberty, in his view, had been closely associated by philosophers with the right to private property. Freedom in the liberal theory of rights was a function of possession. A human being was, by nature, a political animal, 'not only a social animal, but an animal which can develop into an individual only in society'. The philosophers of the Enlightenment had conceived of human beings as isolated individuals competing one with another. Marx did not deny the importance of the individual but believed that the individual could only be assured of his rights when economic and social relationships had been transformed and the causes of injustice had thus been removed. The individual in this ideal, not to say Utopian, social setting would share rights and duties with everyone else.

Whatever the successes or failures of the Soviet system in providing social and economic rights for its citizens, it is repeatedly emphasised in Soviet constitutional documents, in press articles and even in popular songs that the priorities in the provision of rights for Soviet citizens are intended to be education, jobs and leisure rather than liberty, freedom of expression and the right to express dissent from authority. (The latter right seems not to be highly valued within the Soviet Union itself; an opinion poll conducted by a French polling agency in autumn 1987 indicated that, while 73 per cent of the Soviet citizens questioned were in favour of allowing dissidents to leave the country, only 27 per cent were in favour of releasing them back into Soviet society, while 47 per cent actually objected to this.)[4]

It was, therefore, not at all surprising that an attempt by the United States to impose on the Soviet Union the human rights derived from Tom Paine and Thomas Jefferson should be resisted. The Russians resented what they saw as a Western attempt to foist on them a scale of priorities which was not theirs. Their view was expressed in the Russian proverb, 'One does not take one's own rule into another's monastery.' To understand the impact of this, it is not necessary at this stage to enter the debate on the merits of the respective claims of the two systems of human rights; one merely has to consider what effect in Western capitals would have been produced by Soviet demands that, as a condition of Soviet agreement to any arms control proposals from the West, Western governments should agree to reduce their unemployment levels, remove social inequalities, and vastly increase their expenditure on low cost housing, social welfare and health schemes.

The Russians could legitimately claim that they were not the only ones to attach importance to social and economic rights. In his NBC interview on 1st December 1987, Mr Gorbachev reminded his American audience that President Franklin Roosevelt, in his State of the Union Message in January 1944, had declared that certain economic truths had become accepted as self-evident. Roosevelt said:

> We have accepted, so to speak, a second Bill of Rights under which a new basis of security and prosperity can be established for all—regardless of station, race or creed.

As part of this basis of security and prosperity he listed the right to a useful and remunerative job, the right to earn enough to provide adequate food and clothing and recreation, and the right of everyone in business to trade in an atmosphere of freedom from unfair competition. He also spoke of the right of every family to a decent home, the right to medical care, and the right to adequate protection from the economic fears of old age, sickness, accident and unemployment, and the right to good education. But when the President spoke of American preparedness, in the aftermath of the war, to move forward in the implementation of these rights, he seems to have conceived of them first and foremost as rights which should be secured for American citizens rather than rights which belonged naturally to human beings as such. For Roosevelt there was a clear link between human rights and peace:

> America's own rightful place in the world depends in large part upon how fully these and similar rights have been carried into practice for our citizens. For unless there is security at home there cannot be lasting peace in the world.

Roosevelt's speech might, at the height of the struggle of democracy against Nazism and Fascism, be seen as the high tide of idealism. Yet even in that moment, the President did not go so far as to ascribe these economic and social rights to every individual. That he did not do so was a mark of his caution and perhaps also of his wisdom. To ascribe rights to some individuals is to ascribe duties to others, and duties may reasonably be ascribed only in the measure in which those who have them have the ability to fulfil them. Even the wealth and munificence of the United States at that time, and perhaps even subsequently, would hardly have been sufficient to satisfy the claims which such rights would have implied for all the populations of the poorer nations of the earth. The President's speech seems rather to make clear the distinction between aspirations, by which the leaders of the world should be guided in their efforts to provide a better standard of nutrition, health, housing and employment to the citizens of the world, but which require the deployment over a long period of immense human and capital resources, and on the other hand basic political rights, which require no more than that states should pass and enforce legislation which makes the withholding of those rights illegal in their respective territories. It is, of course, true to say that if someone living in one of the poorest lands in Africa has a life expectancy of only 25 years, the economic and social rights ascribed to that person by Roosevelt are more important than the political rights ascribed by Jefferson. But to satisfy the former will take the combined efforts of many nations over many decades, whereas to satisfy the latter requires no more than that the laws of each nation should prohibit the infringement of elementary political rights and that those laws should be fairly and effectively enforced.

Nevertheless, there is still a clear conflict between the concepts of human rights advocated by the Soviet Union and those represented by the tradition of Western thought and most vividly exemplified by Rousseau, Locke, and Tom Paine and by Thomas Jefferson in the Declaration of Independence of the United States. This was the conflict of systems and ideologies which the negotiations at the Helsinki Conference sought to resolve in 1975. That two such disparate conceptions of human rights should be reconciled in a single document was in itself a remarkable feat of diplomacy. In the Final Act of the Helsinki Conference of 1975, that feat was achieved by the devices of juxtaposing apparently conflicting principles in the text and maintaining a balance between them. The principles, all of which are stated to be of equal value, embrace both respect for human rights and fundamental freedoms including the freedom of thought, conscience, religion or belief, and on the other hand the obligation of non-intervention by one state in the internal affairs of another. Thus was preserved the paradox that the United States and its Western partners were able to insist that their interpretation of human rights applied to the citizens of the Soviet Union and other East European countries while the Soviet Union and other states of Eastern Europe were assured that no state intervention in defence of those rights would be permitted from outside.

With human rights thus firmly placed on the agenda of East-West relation, statesmen face difficult choices. Essentially, three possible policy courses are open to them in regard to human rights. First, they can decide that human rights should be excluded altogether from the realm of international discussions on the ground that they obstruct the conduct of business between states and are disruptive of the international order which is based on relations between states which have agreed to respect each other's internal jurisdiction. In other words, states have more important matters to discuss, such as the avoidance of nuclear war and the reduction of levels of armaments, and nothing, not even injustices suffered by individuals, should be allowed to interfere with those discussions. Secondly, at the other end of the scale, it is possible to adopt a policy which sees the interests of the individual as transcending every other moral consideration, even those of peace and disarmament. This is a modern variant of the ancient maxim *fiat justitia ruat caelum*—let justice be done though the heavens shall fall; in other words, the rights of the individual must prevail at whatever cost to the interests of nations. Thirdly, one may attempt to steer a course between these two extremes which, while not allowing human rights to jeopardise the achievement of accord between states on major issues, nevertheless allows some progress to be made over the treatment of individuals, perhaps by small steps and through informal and perhaps even unavowed contacts.

In the world of today it would be neither politically possible nor morally justifiable to ignore the demands that human rights abuses should be corrected, or at least that an attempt should be made to induce other governments to correct them. Few would claim, however, that progress on such global issues as the reduction of armaments or the avoidance of the risk of conflict should take second place to the pursuit through diplomatic channels of justice for an individual who is mistreated by his own government. This unheroic but rational position is clearly stated by R. J. Vincent in the following terms:

> Unless the order which the states enclose, and protect by such instruments as the principle of non-intervention and that of the balance of power, is preserved, then there is no prospect of the achievement of justice for groups and individuals within the state. Order precedes justice. And order in such a rudimentary society as that formed between states is placed under threat if the statesmen make too many demands on it, such as the expectation that it is competent to act in the matter of human rights.[5]

This line of policy pursues the aim of using the levers of diplomatic action not for the sake of improving the lot of this or that victim of the abuse of human rights but in order to secure over the longer term the democratisation of those societies in which human rights abuses occur. This position preserves as axiomatic the notion, shared amongst others by Andrei Sakharov and Henry Kissinger, that the reduction of the danger of nuclear war carries an absolute priority over all other considerations, but it does not abandon the cause of human rights as being an inconvenient interference in the dialogue between governments. It is perhaps against this background that one should interpret the statement of the Soviet Foreign Minister at the conference held in Helsinki in July 1985 to commemorate the tenth anniversary of the CSCE Final Act. On that occasion Mr Shevardnadze said:

> Co-operation between states in the humanitarian fields is thinkable only in conditions of full and strict respect for their sovereignty, laws and administrative regulations, and strict non-interference in internal affairs. This kind of co-operation vitally needs détente and a high level of trust based on stable security.

It is precisely the question of trust which has been at the centre of Western concerns. Since the signature of the Helsinki Final Act and the subsequent charges levelled by other governments against the Soviet government of failing to comply, at least to the satisfaction of its Western partners, with some of the human rights provisions in that document, confidence in the readiness of the

Soviet Union to stand by its undertakings in other matters such as arms control and disarmament has been undermined. For example, Sir Geoffrey Howe, the Foreign and Commonwealth Secretary, speaking at the CSCE meeting in Vienna in November 1986, said:

> Confidence and trust, essential to effective measures of arms control and disarmament, cannot mature in a Europe in which in some countries the rights of ordinary people are ignored.

The resolution of disputes between the Soviet Union and Western governments on human rights cases seems fortunately to have enjoyed the benefit of the same acceleration which has affected progress on major matters of arms control. In the year which saw the achievement of agreement on abolition of medium range and shorter range nuclear missiles, the number of outstanding human rights and family reunification cases in the Soviet Union seemed to have been substantially reduced and the rate of emigration was increased over that of previous years. While further progress is needed, recent decisions of the Soviet government give support to the remarks of the Soviet Foreign Minister quoted above. Notwithstanding this welcome response to Western concerns, there remains a fundamental difference between the two societies about what is meant by the term 'human rights' and what interpretation of that term should prevail in the treatment by governments of the individuals whose destinies they control.

The question from which this chapter began was that of linkage between arms control agreements and insistence on the observance of human rights. Perhaps a change in the international atmosphere is enough to influence the way in which this question is answered. Whereas little more than a year ago it was being argued that arms control agreements should be linked with the insistence on the observance of human rights in the Soviet Union, an arms control agreement of historic importance has been signed in Washington apparently without any linkage to specific human rights conditions. Meanwhile, however, the human rights performance of the Soviet Union is seen to have improved in several respects. The cessation of notorious violations of human rights, for example the confinement of clinically sane dissidents in psychiatric hospitals, is not only a good thing in itself; it also has the merit of taking out of the hands of the opponents of arms control agreements a weapon which they can use to press for their rejection. It has been argued by some that arms control agreements should not be made until the Soviet human rights record improves, but such arguments have been less frequently heard as the rate of emigration of Soviet Jews has increased and as long-standing family reunification cases are resolved. Violations of the human rights provisions agreed in 1975 continue, some of them serious, and they are still a constant source of friction in East-West diplomacy. Equally, the Soviet Union shows no readiness to abate its criticisms of unemployment levels and deprivation in Western societies. But for the arms control process the human rights question is no longer the obstacle which it was in earlier years.

It is precisely the absence of direct linkage which may have facilitated that improvement; but, on the other hand, without the pressures of public opinion in the West it must be seriously doubted whether it would ever have occurred. This is perhaps the strongest reason for keeping the question of human rights in the central place which it has now come to occupy on the international agenda, and for doing so in a more balanced, even-handed and dispassionate way than hitherto. Few countries are immune to the criticism that they have been much more severe in their criticism of human rights abuses by their adversaries than by their friends, and however understandable this may be it remains inconsistent and morally dubious. Human rights questions do, in an important sense, cause us to think about the role of morality in foreign affairs:

> Human rights in foreign policy are not merely about standard-setting, public pronouncements, quiet words with the Minister about particular cases, or finding formulae for the pacification of noisy by unimportant domestic lobbies; they are also matters which affect the great purposes of the state in securing and nourishing its citizens.[6]

There remains, however, the difference noted earlier between the conceptions of human rights propounded and defended by governments and propagandists in West and East alike. Whatever justice there may be in Western accusations of Soviet and East

European denial of political rights (and, for that matter, economic rights) or in Soviet and East European attacks on Western shortcomings, the violation of human rights of both types is horrifyingly widespread in countries which are not members of either grouping, and this is an evil which cries out for remedy.

Christians who seek explicit guidance on human rights in the New Testament find that the Gospels speak to us in the language of duties rather than rights. There is an infinitely greater emphasis on what we should do for others than on what we have a right to expect others to do for us. That we have rights is implied, but often this is by way of exhortation to us to waive those rights for the sake of others. But those rights still exist even though we choose not to exercise them. Secondly, there is all the difference in the world between choosing to waive our own rights and urging others to waive theirs. The expansion of the full enjoyment of those rights by all is the aim which is most consistent with the universality of the love of God towards all people, expressed in the truly epoch-making words of St Paul:

> There is neither Jew nor Greek, there is neither bond nor free, there is neither male nor female; for yet all are one in Christ Jesus.[7]

Summary

In our consideration of the Christian tradition concerning the state and loyalty of citizens to it we noted the balance struck in Christian thought between a recognition and respect for the role of the state and the refusal of Christian thought to absolutise it. This affects the discussion of the place of human rights in the task of making peace in our time. It is clear that the state cannot claim such absolute sovereignty that human rights considerations are totally avoided. However, to make human rights a condition of agreement would be to jeopardise the possibility of peace. In so doing it might also have the effect of hindering the development of more open and democratic life in Eastern Europe and the Soviet Union. The Christian tradition encourages us to support the establishment and protection of both individual and social rights. A proper caution about the desirability of linking human rights issues to the process of détente does not absolve governments from a duty to pursue human rights concerns by other means. The tasks of making peace and of protecting human rights are inextricably interrelated but they may not be best served by making one conditional upon the other.

Footnotes

[1] Hedley Bull: *The Anarchical Society: a Study of Order in World Politics*. Macmillan, 1977, p.83.

[2] *New York Times*, 18th September 1973.

[3] Quoted in Maurice Cranston: *What are Human Rights?* Bodley Head, 1973, p.75.

[4] *Economist*, 7th November 1987, p.44.

[5] R. J. Vincent: *Human Rights and International Relations*. Cambridge University Press in association with Royal Institute of International Affairs, 1986, p.70.

[6] R..J. Vincent: *op. cit.*, p.43.

[7] Galatians 3.28.

6
Third World Conflicts

The Christian Tradition

What, broadly speaking, have conflicts in the Third World been about? How do they relate to Christian ideas of justice and order? Are they quarrels from which we should in all circumstances hold aloof? Can they always be kept distinct from the issues in dispute between the West and the Soviet Union? Are there conflicts arising out of 'national liberation' in, for example, South Africa or Latin America, on which we should take a view and where we should be providing help? How does 'Liberation Theology' relate to these conflicts? It is against the background of answers to such questions as these that the present chapter deals more precisely with some of the political and economic aspects of intervention and arms transfers.

The Christian tradition allows for the possibility both for a 'Just War', and of a 'Just Revolution', but only if certain criteria are fulfilled. One of the criteria has come to be known as the principle of proportion or proportionality. It was first formulated by Thomas Aquinas in his discussion on sedition. There he argued that the attempt to overthrow a tyranny does not count as a sin, unless the attempted overthrow causes the people to suffer more harm than they are having to endure under the unjust rule.[1] This attention to the consequences of revolutionary action was in contrast to the teaching of others before Aquinas who had argued that any tyrant could be struck down and the person who did this was acting as an agent of God. Aquinas's teaching, with its concern for consequences, and its emphasis as much on good order as justice, has been a basic element in Christian teaching on this subject both in the Catholic and Protestant traditions. It brings theological and ethical concerns close to those of the practitioner in the spheres of politics, economics and war.

The Christian tradition, it has to be said, allows for the possibility of just wars of offence, or wars of intervention, where there is a grievous wrong that needs to be put right. In recent years the emphasis in Christian circles, as outside them, has been to allow for only one 'just cause', namely self-defence. But armed intervention, in which one side goes to the help of combatants struggling against an unjust aggressor cannot be totally ruled out by the Christian tradition. But again, the thrust of that tradition, in its best exponents, has been one of extreme caution; a concern to weigh consequences and to ensure, so far as possible, that more harm than good will not ensue.

The Last 40 Years

Over the last 40 years, the global East-West conflict has been experienced in Europe as an 'armed peace' or a 'Cold War'. During the same period, the Third World has experienced armed violence or real war on a considerable scale.

Ruth Sivard[2] estimates that there have been some 105 armed conflicts (defined as deaths of more than 1,000) since the Second World War. All except the Hungarian revolution took place in the Third World. Around 30 million people have died in these wars (compared with approximately 50 million in both World Wars). And millions more have lost their homes, their livelihoods and so on. What is more, the number of wars has been increasing. According to Sivard, there were, on average, nine major wars a year in the 1950s, 11 in the 1960s and 14 per year in the 1970s and 1980s.

Because of the spread of sophisticated weaponry, moreover, wars are becoming more destructive and there are increasing numbers of civilian casualities. For example, one aeroplane carrying cluster munitions, of the type used by Israel in the Lebanon, is said to be equivalent, in immediate destructive effects, to a Lance missile with a single one kiloton nuclear warhead. So far, some 300,000 people have died in the Afghan war, around 400,000 in Iran and Iraq, some 60,000 in El Salvador (more than 1 per cent of the population), around 15,000 in Nicaragua.

Evidently, these wars are the consequence of political and social turbulence in the Third World—a turbulence which arises out of a history of colonialism, uneven development, cultural dislocation, ethnic conflict and a myriad of other factors. Even the term 'Third World' is misleading because it conceals the complexity and variety of societies in Latin America, Africa, the Middle East, the Indian subcontinent and South East Asia. The history of these societies is, of course, interlaced with the history of the developed world; so much so that it is difficult to distinguish between the indigenous causes of war—those rooted in domestic history—from the role and responsibilities of outside powers, both now and in the past. Only a minority of the wars in the Third World can be described as surrogates for the East-West conflict, in the sense that they reproduce the ideological conflict between capitalism and socialism or freedom and totalitarianism, although parties to particular conflicts have often acquired 'East' or 'West' labels owing to their relationship with particular advanced industrial countries.

The emergence of capitalism in the sixteenth and seventeenth centuries marked the beginnings of a global economy and the start of a European colonial process. Today, the economies of those countries, known as the Third World, are deeply entwined with the economies of the advanced industrial countries, while their political and military institutions have been shaped by the heritage of colonialism and by the continuing provision of various forms of assistance from both Western and Socialist countries.

In the aftermath of the Second World War, the United States provided large amounts of economic and military assistance to Third World countries as part of its policy of containing the Soviet Union and China and to assist the development of Third World economies so as to head off domestic discontent and to relieve the former colonial powers of some of their burdens. This assistance did not succeed in creating self-sufficient economies; Third World economies remain heavily dependent on the West for markets and for technology and credits. Only a few newly industrialising countries (South Korea, Taiwan, etc.) managed to break through into world manufacturing markets.

The process of development brought good and bad consequences. Economic growth expanded the towns and newly created middle classes. Agricultural as well as industrial production increased, especially after the so-called Green revolution of the 1960s. However, as more and more production was oriented towards world markets, traditional livelihoods, resources, and social and cultural relationships were often destroyed and new inequalities were created between town and country, region and region, nation and nation. Conflicts over resources and over economic and cultural exploitation were added to more long-standing disputes, arising from communal rivalries, the departure of colonial powers, and the redrawing of maps after the Second World War. Given the dependence on the West, it was not surprising that movements in the Third World struggling to change their societies tended to attribute their ills to the West and to look to the Soviet Union as an alternative.

The connections between the Soviet Union and Third World countries were always much less than those of the West. Russia had expanded westward and eastward, rather than southward, although the Western countries were always nervous about Russian interests in the Near East. Nevertheless, the empire inherited and consolidated by the Bolsheviks was a continental empire. During the Stalinist period which was characterised by the two camp doctrine, economic and military assistance was only provided to socialist developing countries, like China, North Korea and North Vietnam. This policy changed under Khrushchev, when Third World regimes were recognised as progressive bourgeois nationalist governments. The first intimation of change was the economic assistance signed with Egypt in 1954. During this period, assistance was provided to Third World countries wishing to reduce their dependence on the West, even when, in some cases, domestic communist parties were suppressed. Soviet policy became more interventionist in the 1970s, with the spread of new 'post-revolutionary' regimes in Indo-China, Southern Africa, Ethiopia and the Yemen, all of which demanded and received Soviet assistance.

In recent years, Soviet policy seems to have changed again. Soviet writers point out that there have been many Soviet failures, most notably in Egypt, that the Soviet model is not necessarily the correct model for Third World countries, and that Soviet assistance has not succeeded in reducing Third World dependence on the West. As of 1985, only some 3.6 per cent of the exports of the average Third World country (excluding socialist developing countries) go to European socialist countries (including the Soviet Union) and only 2.5 per cent of imports come from those countries.

Obviously, peacekeeping in the Third World is an immensely complicated problem, which cannot be discussed in a few pages. Each conflict has a unique history which has to be studied and understood in its own right. Because the East-West conflict is global in an ideological and military sense, we are able to generalise about peacemaking across the East-West divide. In contrast, Third World conflicts tend to be specific and particular. It is in the Third World context that liberation theology has played such a significant role.

Liberation theology works on the assumption that God is ceaselessly at work liberating human beings from all that oppresses them, not just personally but in the political, economic and social spheres in which their lives are set and by which they are shaped. Many Christians today share this perspective. But this perspective by itself does not tell us whether or not we should support the Afghan rebels or Savunda's South African backed forces in Mozambique, or the African National Congress (ANC), or the Sandinista government in Nicaragua, or South West Africa People's Organisation (SWAPO) and so on. It is not possible to move from liberation theology, even with its commitment to the poor (for the poor need order as well as justice) straight to judgements about particular revolutionary movements or governments. Ethical reflection and political and economic analysis must first take place. This chapter does not claim to offer general guidance on how to assess the justice of any particular war or revolution in the third world; that would require a much more lengthy and detailed treatise. Rather, it focuses on two general issues—the arms trade and military intervention—which are the most obvious connections between the Cold War in Europe and third world conflicts. It has its setting within a Christian perspective in which God has a particular concern for those whom Franz Fanon once described as 'the wretched of the earth' and for their economic, political and human development.

The Nature of the Connections Between Cold and Hot Wars

The first and most obvious connection is direct and indirect military intervention by the superpowers and by former colonial countries like Britain and France. The Soviet invasion in Afghanistan, the American attack on Libya, the French role in Chad are all examples of direct intervention, i.e. the military involvement of outside forces in Third World conflicts. In addition, the US especially has stepped up covert or indirect intervention, i.e. the use of special operatives, military 'advisers', the CIA, etc., in Third World conflicts, under the so-called Reagan doctrine,[3] as in the case of the support provided to the Contras in Nicaragua. It has been estimated that since the Second World War, the US has directly intervened in roughly a quarter of the wars in the Third World since 1945 and the former colonial powers in more than a third.[4]

On the Western side, there seems to be some correspondence between the Cold War and the level of intervention. During the détente period of the 1970s, there seems to have been a tendency to retreat from intervention. This followed the debacle in Vietnam and the end of the decolonisation process.

During the early 1980s, however, intervention seemed to be on the increase again. The Reagan Doctrine calls for increased support for right-wing governments facing radical insurgencies (known as 'terrorists') and for insurgents (known as 'freedom fighters') fighting against left-wing regimes.

The infrastructure and strategies of intervention have been built up during this period. The Carter Administration established the Rapid Deployment Force in 1980 and negotiated bases for it in Morocco, Egypt, Oman, Somalia and Kenya. Under Reagan it was renamed US CENTCOM (US Central Command). It now numbers around a quarter of a million men and was involved in Grenada, Lebanon, the bombing of Libya and now the Gulf. European powers have also increased their intervention forces. France retains a network of bases and facilities in sub-Saharan Africa. During the 1960s and 1970s, French troops overseas were reduced. However, since 1981 France has created the Force d'Action Rapide (FAR) with 47,000 men, based in France, as a mobile intervention force both for Central Europe and for the Third World.

Britain, likewise, withdrew forces during the 1960s and 1970s, especially after the decision to withdraw East of Suez in 1966. Since the Falklands War, Britain has established its own intervention force, based on the Fifth Airborne Brigade of Paratroops and the Third Commando Brigade Royal Marines.[5]

During the 1980s, the US has also adopted new military strategies which are intended both for Europe and Third World. These strategies—Airland Battle in the case of the Army, and the Maritime Strategy in the case of the Navy—emphasise offensive doctrines, forward deployment, the integration of nuclear and conventional planning, mobility and visibility. According to a Pentagon official:

> What was needed for the 1980s and beyond was flexibility—in doctrine, in mobility, in responsiveness—rather than continued concentration upon the European theatre as a separate and dominant entity.[6]

Although NATO has not formally adopted either of the strategies, European countries are increasingly involved in their implementation. For the Americans, this renewed emphasis on intervention is explicitly seen in Cold War terms. First of all, there are cases in which intervention is directly viewed as a way of countering insurgences or opposing governments which are thought to be backed by the Soviet Union. Secondly, intervention may be intended to secure strategic objectives, like freedom of the seas or access to overseas bases, which contribute to an overall global strategy, in which deterrence in Europe is one component.

The European powers tend to be more pragmatic in their objectives—emphasising practical aims like access to oil or responsibility to former colonies as well as wider East-West considerations.

On the Soviet side, intervention appears to have increased during the 1970s and 1980s. The Afghan war is the only post-war example of direct intervention by Soviet forces outside Europe. However, indirect support to post-revolutionary regimes in Southern Africa, the Horn of Africa and Indo-China increased in the 1970s. Since the 1960s, the Soviet Union has deployed its naval forces in the Mediterranean and the Indian Ocean and recently acquired its first overseas naval base at the former US base in Cam Ranh bay, Vietnam. There is some evidence now that the Soviet Union sees the focus of strategic interest shifting from Europe to South West Asia. It would be wrong, however, to argue that it was the 'weakness' of the West that allowed the Soviet Union to increase its overseas role, even though the Soviet Union itself uses a similar argument. In the 1970s, Soviet analysts argued that the Soviet overseas role contributed to the achievement of 'parity' which provided the conditions for détente.

Rather, the increased Soviet role reflects internal developments within the Third World—the emergence of left-wing regimes which turn to the Soviet Union as an alternative to dependence on the West. Of course, it is true that the emergence of such regimes reflects the decline of Western influence. But it is not at all clear that this decline can be reversed through military means nor is it clear that the Soviet Union is faring any better than the West.

A second set of connections is established through arms transfers. According to US State Department figures, arms transfers reached a peak of $40 billion in 1982.[7] Of these, some $33 billion, or 80 per cent, went to developing countries. Subsequently, arms transfers have declined quite dramatically. By 1985, arms transfers to developing countries had declined by approximately one-third, to $22 billion. There was no significant decrease in arms transfers within the industrialised world.

The reasons for the decline are mainly economic. The credit and oil boom of the 1970s increased orders for major weapons systems which were delivered in the late 1970s and early 1980s. Arms transfers were explicitly seen as a way of recycling petrodollars. Indeed, arms are an important source of foreign exchange for both the United States and the Soviet Union. Growing indebtedness in the early 1980s (high interest rates and declining commodity prices) has dramatically reduced the demand for weapons.

But it is also possible to speculate about political reasons, arising from the link between the superpower arms race and arms races in the Third World. There seems to have been, over the last

40 years, an inverse relationship between intervention and arms trade, and between domestic arms procurement and arms trade.[8] There are several possible explanations for this relationship. First of all, the superpowers, and especially the United States, may be readier to restrain the transfer of arms in situations where they themselves are likely to intervene. But more importantly, they are likely to promote arms transfers as a political instrument when they are unwilling to intervene directly. This was the essence of the Nixon Doctrine. Nixon's Secretary of Defence, Clark Clifford, made it clear on several occasions that it is cheaper and safer to arm a Third World soldier than to intervene directly with an American soldier.

Secondly, arms producers, especially European countries, are dependent on arms exports to maintain capacity in the arms industry. The levelling off of military spending in the early 1970s, in the West, led to increased export promotion efforts to compensate for the decline in domestic orders. This was mitigated somewhat in the early 1980s by real increases in arms procurement budgets. Nevertheless, arms companies are still heavily dependent on arms exports. And the decline in arms exports has contributed to budgetary pressures, especially in Britain and Italy. The desperation of arms companies is indicated by recent scandals about illegal exports to Iran and Iraq, especially in Sweden and Italy.

The Soviet Union, the United States and Western Europe account for around 80 per cent of the total arms trade. The Soviet Union, according to US State Department figures, is the leading supplier, accounting for nearly 30 per cent of the total, although Soviet supplies are much more concentrated on a few recipients than US and West European supplies. (According to Stockholm International Peace Research Institute (SIPRI) figures, the Soviet Union lags slightly behind the United States.)[9]

The United States accounts for a further 26 per cent of the total, while West European suppliers account for around 24 per cent. West European arms exports declined in the 1950s and 1960s as the superpowers replaced their political roles in the Third World. In the 1970s and 1980s, arms exports have increased again as a way of offsetting the cost of maintaining a domestic arms industry.

This is especially true in France where arms exports account for a substantial share of total production.

Third World arms production is also increasing although Third World arms producers remain heavily dependent on imported parts and know-how. Brazil and Israel are becoming significant exporters of arms.

Arms transfers and military interventions probably constitute the most important connections between the arms competition in Europe and conflicts in the Third World. But many other connections should be mentioned. These include military assistance training; sharing of intelligence which has become more important as the technology of intelligence has developed; joint military exercises especially in Latin America and the Far East—the sale of commercial nuclear reactors, which, despite the Non-Proliferation Treaty, facilitates the proliferation of nuclear capabilities.

The Consequences

It is possible to distinguish two main consequences of military intervention and arms transfers for Third World conflicts—the direct effects on war in the Third World, and the indirect effects on the underlying causes of conflict.

In the early postwar years, there were several examples of situations in which military intervention, in Third World areas, was relatively successful in achieving its political objectives—establishing pro-western regimes and restoring stability. Greece and Turkey, Malaysia, the Philippines (in the 1950s) are regularly cited. But the subsequent record suggests that this is no longer the case. Military intervention, and to a lesser extent, arms transfers can be used to destabilise particular political situations, as in Nicaragua, Angola, or the Lebanon, and may prolong or increase the destructiveness of conflicts. But they are relatively unsuccessful in controlling conflicts or in influencing the political composition of governments, except in very minor instances. Grenada and the Falklands war might be considered examples in which the intervening forces achieved their immediate political objectives. But both cases were relatively costly in terms of military resources and the political situation remains unresolved.

There are several reasons for the unsatisfactoriness of military intervention as an instrument of policy. One is the arms trade itself. In contrast to the days of gunboat diplomacy, advanced industrial countries face Third World opponents equipped with a similar vintage of armaments. A second reason is the spread of the nation-state and the mobilising appeal of nationalist ideas. And a third reason is the deep-rooted nature of the Cold War itself. Any intervention by a superpower, or one of its allies, tends to draw what may be a local and perhaps particular conflict into a global project. The consequence is to polarise the conflict, giving both East and West an interest in avoiding the defeat of one side or another, as in Central America, Southern Africa, the Horn of Africa or Afghanistan.

Nor is this peculiarly a Western problem. The Soviet Union faced a similar plight in Afghanistan. There is some evidence that the domestic unpopularity of the Afghan war in the Soviet Union was one of the factors influencing the Gorbachev reforms.*

Robin Luckham has argued:[10]

> The fact is that the inability of the major world powers to control events in the Third World has been time and again decisively demonstrated. Hence, there is a surreal quality about their creation of vast military apparatuses for Third World intervention. These add to the influence of the major powers only so long as they are confined to minor or symbolic engagements in which there is little risk of failure. But the more such apparatuses are built up, the greater is the temptation to ignore such limitations and risk the escalation of conflict beyond the major powers' capacity to control it.

The various military ties that link the advanced industrial world to the Third World also have indirect consequences for the domestic political and economic structures in Third World countries, which may cause or exacerbate conflict. The arms

---

* A film is currently showing to large audiences in the Soviet Union called 'It's Not Easy to be Young'. The film shows interviews with Afghan veterans—their difficulty in adapting to Soviet life after their experience of the fact that they are not treated as heroes—which is very reminiscent of the Vietnam war veterans. At the European Nuclear Disarmament Convention in Coventry, some Soviet officials, often in disagreement with their colleagues, were arguing that the invasion of Afghanistan was a tragic mistake.

trade especially has had a profound influence on the direction of development in Third World countries. While the evidence as to whether military intervention, arms trade, or military spending contributes to economic growth is, to say the least, ambiguous,[11] there does seem to be a relationship between these phenomena and the growth of industrial enclaves which are also associated with growing inequalities between town and country, regions, social classes and ethnic groups, with the degradation of the environment, and consequently, with the suppression of traditional cultures and ways of life.

It used to be fashionable, in the 1950s and 1960s, to argue that the armed forces were the spearhead of 'modernisation' and 'Westernisation'. The provision of military assistance, training and arms trade, created local armed forces on the model of advanced industrial countries. This did not mean that such armies were pro-Western or pro-Soviet. But it did mean that these armed forces had a vested interest in creating an industrial infrastructure in which modern armaments could be operated effectively. Moreover, because the armed forces were often the most cohesive and well organised institution in many of these new states, they were able to exert considerable political influence. For these reasons, the drive for industrialisation often took precedence over the needs of the poorest people, who lacked what Amartya Sen calls 'entitlements'.

The acquisition of modern armaments or the construction of a foreign base creates a chain of supplementary demands, for airfields, roads, telephones, radar systems, repair shops, special skills, spare parts, special types of materials, especially steel and petroleum products. These infrastructural demands, especially where domestic arms manufacture is undertaken, can provide an important impetus for industrialisation, although it is the type of industrialisation that is characteristic of arms production in rich countries. It is capital-intensive, import-intensive and skill-intensive. Arms imports account for an extremely high share of capital imports. The cost of a job in the arms industry or related industry is much higher in terms of foreign exchange than a job in civilian industry or agriculture and requires highly specialised skills.

To pay for this type of industrialisation, Third World countries must obtain foreign exchange, either through grants or loans, or through the export of primary products. The consequent impoverishment of the countryside is a well-known phenomenon. More and more commodities are produced for urban and world markets instead of subsistence. Yet income is often insufficient to feed the producers. Poor farmers are squeezed out by the introduction of more efficient methods of production, worsening terms of trade, or the import of cheap food from industrialised countries. Cheap labour is drawn into the towns where jobs are scarce because industrialisation is so capital-intensive. It is not at all clear that industrialisation can generate sufficient growth to compensate for this massive social, economic and cultural dislocation, because it is so difficult to compete on world markets for advanced technology products. The increase in interest rates and the fall in commodity prices in the 1980s has exacerbated these tendencies.

The consequence of what is often known as uneven development is conflict and/or oppression. Very often, the military intervene to 'manage' the consequences of uneven development and sustain the emphasis on industrialisation. Indeed, Ruth Sivard has shown that over the post-war period, there has been a steady increase in military-controlled governments in the Third World. In 1960, some 28 per cent of the independent Third World states were controlled by the military. In 1986, this figure had risen to 50 per cent. Military-controlled governments are associated with greater repression and with the deprivation of political rights, suppressing potential conflicts and possibly storing up the conditions for war in the future.[11]

Towards a Peacemaking Role in the Third World

Whether or not deterrence has kept the peace in Europe, the components of deterrence—competitive armaments and a Cold War ideology—are linked to wars and violence in the Third World. It is probably exaggerated to argue that stability in Europe has been purchased at the cost of instability in the Third World, but when we congratulate ourselves for the post-war situation in

Europe, we should take into account the situation in the poorest parts of the world, in which we are involved and have some responsibility.

Western political objectives for direct and indirect intervention (via arms transfers or military advice) can be broadly summarised under two headings. First, the West has attempted to prevent the spread of, mainly, left-wing insurgences, to stem the tide of totalitarianism. Secondly intervention has been directed at certain strategic goals, like access to oil or to naval facilities.

The problem with the first set of objectives is that the methods used to combat insurgences may often contribute to the problem. It is true that revolutions in places like Cuba or Vietnam have established oppressive regimes. However, Western attempts to counter these developments often result in regimes that are equally oppressive. Military intervention and arms trade have directly, or indirectly through the structural effects on uneven development, contributed to military governments and to dictatorships. There is not much to choose between dictatorships and totalitarian regimes. Dictatorships may offer more cultural and political space: the state is less pervasive. However, punishments are often more brutal (torture, executions, etc.) and extremes of wealth and poverty are much greater.

Western military intervention, especially since Vietnam, has often increased rather than decreased instability. Intervention, whether direct or indirect, has tended to raise the level of violence through the increased availability of destructive military equipment, and to exacerbate the underlying causes of conflicts, both because of the cost of military equipment and because it has tended to polarise and entrench conflictual positions. The same can be said of Soviet intervention, as can be seen in Afghanistan.

As for the second set of objectives, securing certain strategic aims, these have to be weighed against the consequences for the local situation. Do these objectives justify the use of violence? Can oil, for example, be secured without inflicting casualties or without other consequences—economic inequality, oppression, etc?

A good example, in this respect, is the Gulf War. First, which is a more important objective: ending the war in the Gulf or ensuring the principle of free access to international waters? If it is the case that these two objectives contradict each other, i.e. that ensuring access to the Gulf maintains oil revenues which allow the war to be prolonged, should not the goal of peacemaking have precedence over access to oil? Should we not tighten our belts in order to bring an end to the war? Or alternatively, is the principle of freedom of the seas so important as to override the continuing suffering in the war?

Secondly, if it is thought important to ensure freedom of the seas, either because it does not conflict with the goal of peace-keeping, or because the principle is considered overriding, what is the best way to ensure access to the Gulf? It can be argued that it is wrong for the West to undertake to uphold this global principle, unilaterally. It raises suspicions in the Third World that Western goals are not as magnanimous as claimed, that the West is using global principles to gain Western military advantages. Secondly, it risks an East-West polarisation of the Gulf War. Because the West is seen to be favouring Iraq, the Soviet Union may come out in favour of Iran, turning the victims of the war into footballs of the Cold War. Hence, such intervention needs to be even-handed, as between Iraq and Iran, and ought to involve East-West co-operation, preferably under the aegis of the United Nations. The UN Security Council Resolution 598 is an example of such possible co-operation.

Of course, all such situations are very complicated and whatever the West does has consequences. Not intervening, standing back, from a war like that in the Gulf, as indeed has been the attitude of many Western countries until recently, also has consequences which are not entirely beneficial: it is a way of tolerating a situation which ought not to be tolerated. In a way there is a parallel here with our relationships in Europe. It is clearly wrong and dangerous to contemplate the use of military force to correct human rights abuses in Eastern Europe: but this does not mean that we should adopt the opposite position of tolerating such abuses (see Chapter 3). In the Third World, the circumstances in which direct or indirect military intervention is justified are extremely limited but, again, that does not mean that we should tolerate injustice, violence and poverty in the Third

World. Hence, what we are discussing is forms of involvement, methods of trying to deal with difficult situations.

The following implications can be drawn from this argument.

First, direct military intervention is almost always counter-productive and should be avoided, except in the context of UN peacekeeping. This is especially important for a country like Britain which can rarely afford to carry the burden of unilateral intervention, and ought to be careful about participation in a NATO or West European framework because of the danger of globalising the Cold War. Secondly, any transfer of arms needs to be justified in terms of very clear political objectives in which concern about justice or peacemaking in the Third World has priority over purely strategic or economic concerns. Indeed arms transfers for purely economic motives ought to be avoided. Such an approach implies much greater restrictions on arms sales. In place of the current policy that arms sales are by and large allowed and even encouraged, where they do not conflict with important policy objectives, a country like Britain ought to take an opposite position, that arms sales are by and large forbidden, except where there are important policy objectives.

It is worth noting that Britain does have a stricter set of guidelines governing the transfer of arms than, say, France or Italy. While there are no legal rules, however, there has been selective control or restraint to countries at war, or close to war, and to countries violating human rights. These guidelines do seem to have constrained the arms trade at least during the 1970s, a period of boom. Nevertheless, in recent years, the active promotional policy of the Ministry of Defence has resulted in an *increase* in arms sales since the mid-1980s, despite the global decrease in arms sales.

There is an argument for opposing all commercial *sales* of arms on the grounds that these tend to be motivated by economic considerations. They imply that violence is peddled for profit. This approach would not, of course, preclude military assistance —gratis arms transfers or sales on favourable terms in situations where we have a strong political commitment, say the defence of Tanzania against South African incursions. A milder form of restriction, adopted by Sweden, West Germany, Japan and a number of other countries, is to ban on a legal basis arms sales to countries at war or countries with repressive regimes. The problem, of course, is implementation, as vividly illustrated in the Bofors scandal and the recent West German deals with South Africa.

Some Third World governments argue that restrictions on arms sales are discriminatory. They should have the right to purchase arms in order to redress military inequality. There is, of course, something in the argument: the acquisition of sophisticated arms by Third World countries has blunted the effectiveness of military intervention. Nevertheless, it can also be argued that the acquisition of arms increases dependence and economic inequality and these are what matter today in the global political hierarchy. Indeed, one could go further and argue the ability *not* to buy weapons is a form of leverage possessed by Third World countries.

Thirdly, we should try to facilitate various regional security arrangements that have been proposed in recent years. These include nuclear-free zones (as in Latin America and in the Pacific), zones of peace and security (as in the Indian Ocean and Latin America), regional arms limitation accords (as in the Ayacucho Agreement of 1974), mutual defence and non-aggression pacts, and so on. If requested, Britain could also play a more active independent peacemaking role in conflicts involving the superpowers, e.g. Central America or Afghanistan.

In this connection, there is a particular role that Churches could play in bringing together and supporting non-governmental organisations and social groups who are interested in peace-keeping and who could exert influence within their societies. Pax Christi, in the Netherlands, has played a pioneering role in this respect—bringing together, for example, moderate Palestinians and Israelis (see Chapter 11).

There are, of course, other proposals that could be put forward: stricter controls on nuclear proliferation together with support for alternative energy sources, more progressive aid policies which are directed at the poorest people, and so on. But all these proposals are quite difficult to carry out without détente, reconciliation and arms limitation in Europe. So long as the Cold War persists between the superpowers, Third World conflicts will often be cast in Cold War terms, thereby justifying intervention by the superpowers, or their allies. So long as advanced industrial countries, especially European countries, manufacture arms, the pressure to export arms for economic reasons will seem compelling and ways will be found to overcome restrictions.

This does not mean that détente and reconciliation will necessarily reduce conflict, violence and outside intervention in the Third World. On the contrary, it is possible to draw up quite a different scenario. Insofar as military and industrial institutions in both East and West exert an autonomous pressure on governments, then détente in Europe could encourage a search for new 'threats' to justify maintaining levels of military spending and could increase the pressure to sell arms. And in the long run, such a scenario could threaten détente in Europe, as well, by setting in motion a new military competition in the Third World. That is why it is so important that peacemaking in Europe should be accompanied by a positive programme for peacemaking in the Third World. Détente and reconciliation is a necessary condition for peacemaking in the Third World, and by no means a sufficient condition. What is more, continued instability in the Third World could undermine détente and reconciliation in Europe.

Obviously, the main opportunities for peacemaking are to be found within the Third World itself. The argument could perhaps be presented the other way round. When the Iranian revolution resulted in the cancellation of substantial arms orders from Britain and Italy, this led to considerable budgetary pressure and stimulated interest among trade unionists in the conversion of arms industries. Already the decline in the arms trade has created industrial pressures for new procurement, which may contribute to budgetary crises in European countries, causing, along with other factors, a re-examination of the relative importance of conventional and nuclear forces, and of procurement and manpower, as well as changes in methods of procurement. It could be that peacemaking within the Third World could be an important way of contributing to peacemaking within Europe.

Summary

This chapter points to the complexity of the relationships of conflicts in the Third World to the East-West divide. We need to avoid a single cause and effect argument which links the various conflicts in the Third World to the struggle between the super-powers. In an interdependent world there are connections. It would be wrong, however, to see the one as the result of the other. Nevertheless, there are things which can be done in both East and West which would help in the management and control of conflict elsewhere. Avoidance of military intervention, except in the context of UN peacekeeping, and careful policies for the control of arms transfer are two important examples of this. Furthermore, we believe that the pursuit of détente and of peaceful relationships between East and West can only have beneficial effects on the work of making and keeping peace elsewhere in the world.

Footnotes

[1] See Richard Harries, *Should Christians support Guerillas*. Lutterworth, 1982.

[2] Ruth Leger Sivard, *World Military and Social Expenditures, 1985*. World Priorities, Washington DC, 1985.

[3] See Fred Halliday, *Beyond Irangate: The Reagan Doctrine and the Third World*. Transnational Institute, Amsterdam 1986.

[4] Robin Luckham, 'Europe, NATO and the Third World: Can they be Dealigned?' in Mary Kaldor and Richard Falk (eds), *Dealignment: A New Foreign Policy Perspective*. Basil Blackwell, Oxford 1987.

[5] See 'Outside the NATO Area', in *Statement on the Defence Estimates, 1987*. Cm 101-0, HMSO, London 1987, pp.22–24.

[6] Quoted in Luckham, *op cit*, fn 3, p.211.

[7] US Arms Control and Disarmament Agency, *World Military Expenditures and Arms Transfers, 1986*. Washington DC, April 1987.

[8] The argument is advanced in Stockholm International Peace Research Institute, *The Arms Trade with the Third World*. Stockholm 1971, Chapter 1.

[9] Stockholm International Peace Research Institute, *World Armaments and Disarmament: SIPRI Yearbook 1987*. Oxford University Press, 1987.

[10] Luckham, *op cit*, fn 3, p.249.

[11] See, for example, R. Faini, P. Annex and L. Taylor, 'Defense Spending Economic Structure and Growth: Evidence Among Countries Over Time', *Economic Development and Cultural Change*, 1984; Saadet Deger, *Military Expenditure in Third World Countries: The Economic Effects*. London: Routledge and Kegan Paul, 1986.

[12] Ruth Leger Sivard, *World Military and Social Expenditures, 1986*. World Priorities, Washington DC, 1986.

7
Perspectives for the Future

Fortunately, perhaps, for those who attempt to predict the course of future international developments, few people bother in later years to check the accuracy of their forecasts. If the forecasts turn out to have been reasonably correct, the forecaster himself will find it difficult to resist the temptation to draw attention to his success. While such success may be due to the unusual perspicacity of an individual, it is at least as likely to be the result of good luck; for if anything is likely to be true of the future, it is that it will not be a mere extrapolation of the trends of the past. St Paul may not have been using the word in our present-day sense when he wrote that where there be prophecies they shall fail, but the many unsuccessful attempts to predict the future give his remark in retrospect a depressing degree of wisdom.

An attempt to forecast the development of East-West relations made only five years ago would inevitably have centred on the prospects for the leadership of the Soviet Union. Were the elderly and cautious men directing the affairs of the Soviet Union prepared to negotiate seriously and in detail with the United States and its partners to begin reducing the nuclear and conventional forces of the two sides? Would they recognise the urgency of taking radical action to stir the stagnant economy of the Soviet Union and to give it the vitality to meet the needs of a superpower? Would it become easier for anyone in the West, or indeed in the East, to find out what was really going on in the Soviet Union? Experts were on the alert for signs of change but, at least in the aftermath of the death of President Brezhnev in November 1982, there were few who would have answered any of these questions with an unequivocal affirmative. When the main cause of dispute between East and West was deployment of

Cruise and Pershing II missiles, for which the leaders of the basing countries in Europe had withstood much domestic criticism, it would have been foolhardy to predict that within five years the removal of these missiles would begin and simultaneously the removal of a much larger number of Soviet missiles.

Everyone knows that these developments have taken place since the advent to power of Mr Gorbachev in the Soviet Union, and that he himself has proclaimed the connection between the 'new thinking' in Soviet foreign policy and the urgent need to restructure the Soviet economy. A bold new approach to these problems was made necessary, as Soviet economists now frankly declare, by the failure during the stagnant years to undertake the necessary reforms. But there may also have been an element of challenge and response. The landslide victory in 1980 of President Ronald Reagan signalled more than a shift to the right in American public opinion. It marked a turning away from the path that was meant to lead on from the SALT II agreement to a SALT III agreement, a sharp increase in US defence appropriations and a raising of the level of rhetoric in which the policies of the Soviet Union were denounced. Some in Moscow seem to have been under the impression that these developments increased the danger of a Third World War; it is probable, however, that these indications of renewed assertiveness in US policy served the useful purpose of heightening the sense in Moscow that changes had become overdue.

Despite the growing importance of areas outside the territories of the NATO and Warsaw Pact countries, notably those on the Western rim of the Pacific Ocean, in the remaining years of the present century and beyond it the most important relationship is likely still to be that between the system of market economy and what has hitherto been known as the system of centrally controlled economies. It is already clear that the processes of economic restructuring in the economies of the East European countries will move at different speeds, and reform will be embraced with different degrees of enthusiasm and energy in each country. Its complete triumph might ultimately make 'centrally controlled economies' a misnomer; but for the present it seems safe to assume that the familiar division of Europe into groupings of states with quite clearly distinct forms of economic organisation will persist well into the twenty-first century.

As long as these two groupings, with their economic and political links, remain in broadly their present form, it is unlikely that the military organisations which are the symptoms rather than the cause of the confrontation between them will dissolve. Like the state in Karl Marx's theoretical structure, the alliances will melt away when there are no longer sufficient reasons for their continuing existence. For the foreseeable future, however, the states of Western and Eastern Europe alike will face the need to provide for their security, and far-reaching changes will be needed in policies and attitudes before there is any realistic prospect that they will rely on any means other than collective security. The needs of collective security will mean that for the time being we shall still find ourselves living with the existing alliance systems. But in the aftermath of the 1987 Washington treaty which is to lead to the abolition of an entire class of land-based nuclear weapons, the confrontation of the two alliances is likely to change. The members of both alliances have already recognised the importance of securing by negotiation a reduction of the levels of strategic nuclear missiles in the arsenals of the USSR and the USA. This difficult but vital US-Soviet negotiation is in 1988 the focus of hopes and prayers that the change in the international climate which began in Washington in December 1987 will continue and that in that climate new arms control measures will be agreed.

The continued existence of the two alliances is compatible with a renewed and serious effort to cut down the conventional forces of each to levels which, given recent indications of Soviet readiness to contemplate 'asymmetrical' reductions, could also result in a much more stable balance between East and West. Measures to improve confidence (discussed in Chapter 10) could have the effect of reducing the risk that innocuous movements of ships, aircraft or troops will be perceived as evidence of aggressive intent. Efforts to reduce, by negotiation, the level of confrontation and to change the perception of threats, however much both are to be valued, will not remove the need for adequate security arrangements in the eyes of the Soviet Union or the nations of the

West. Rapid and unforeseen changes in the character and style of leadership in Moscow and Washington have occurred often enough over the last 40 years, and there is no reason to believe that they will not recur. The framework of security must be strong enough to accommodate domestic changes in the major nations and must be stable over a long period of time. It has to last beyond the next US presidential election or the next Congress of the Communist Party of the Soviet Union.

The United States

The early 1980s were the years in which the United States enjoyed a period of renewal after the long anguish and frustration of the Vietnam years and the shock and embarrassment of Watergate. Sustained economic growth, increased military strength and a belief that in the Soviet Union economic problems and irresolute leadership by old men had caused a relative weakening and loss of nerve combined to give the US a new freedom of manoeuvre in its global foreign policy. Soviet difficulties in Afghanistan, South Yemen and parts of Africa coincided in time with American foreign interventions in Grenada and Libya which, despite much criticism abroad, achieved their objectives. America, it appeared, had regained the initiative. Its leaders felt able to claim that the political and economic system of which it was and is the largest and strongest representative would eventually prevail in the global contest of ideas and power with the Soviet system. Influential people in some quarters in the US argued that arms control concessions or modification of rules limiting the transfer of technology to the Soviet bloc were needless compromises which would support and legitimise an unsatisfactory status quo. If the Soviet Union wished to gain the benefits of co-operation with advanced Western countries in the new phase of economic development based on computer-controlled technologies in an 'information society' whose organisational and financial base is global, said the advocates of this view, then the Soviet Union should reduce its vast defence effort and liberalise its economy and society.

Against this ebullient view, the opinion of many in the liberal establishment, which had in the pre-Reagan years been dominant in the US and which still enjoyed wide support in Western Europe, insisted that mutual security could and should be achieved at a lower level of armed strength. Such people were convinced that, whatever the motives and aspirations of the Soviet Union might be, it would always be sensible and in American as well as in European interests to achieve agreements (provided that the West could drive hard bargains) on arms control and other matters with the Russians. To allow this opportunity to pass by was to condemn the world to a further period of sterile and dangerous East-West confrontation.

Both schools of thought have some inconvenient facts to deal with. The Russians in general and Mr Gorbachev in particular are not as gloomy about their prospects as Western observers think they should be. The weakness of the dollar and the stock market collapse of October 1987 seemed to vindicate those who had argued that, despite America's economic strength, the huge budget deficit called for cuts in US government expenditure, especially on defence. US industry complains of its vulnerability to foreign competition and finance from overseas plays a larger role than formerly in the US economy. Increased economic competition in the US domestic market from the European Community, Japan and the newly industrialising countries arouse protectionist instincts. Feelings of irritation at European allies who are believed, often quite unfairly, not to be 'pulling their weight' and making an adequate contribution to the costs of defence, reinforce such tendencies. The resulting mood could eventually produce a weary turning away from the problems of Europe, especially if relations between the Soviet Union, China and Japan enter a more active phase. Although progress has not been dramatic, an improvement of its relations with both China and Japan has become an important objective of the Soviet Union. The significance of the process of reform in China and China's relationship with the US needs no underlining. Even now, the rising importance to the United States of the Pacific basin is evident in economic terms; North America's trade with Asia is greater than its trade with Europe.

The philosophy of the traditional liberal establishment has a strong appeal among a broad spectrum of American voters. If in the earlier 1980s it was in eclipse, the setbacks which the US administration suffered in 1987, together with the rapid development of a new relationship with Moscow, might well open new perspectives for it.

These two lines of thought on the conduct of East-West relations are still discernible, despite the spectacular changes in US-Soviet relations. To put them in perspective we must consider the changes taking place in the Soviet Union.

The Soviet Union

Like Czarist Russia before it, the Soviet Union has experienced alternating periods of rapid transformations followed by immobility. After 20 years of stagnation it is now obvious that startling changes are occurring in many areas of Soviet life, from the organisation of industry and foreign trade to the realm of literature and art. For the first year following Mr Gorbachev's assumption of the office of Secretary General of the Communist Party of the Soviet Union, it was too early to assess with confidence the significance of the changes he was making. Were they the precursors of the much more profound structural changes required for genuine modernisation of the Soviet economy, or were they, like other much heralded reforms in the past, changes of style—yet one more attempt to tinker with the existing economic machinery in the hope that it could be made to work more efficiently?

Whatever questions there may be about the eventual result of the new revolution which Mr Gorbachev has launched, two things are certain. The attention of the world is more intently focused on the politics of the Soviet Union than at any time in the past three decades; and secondly, whatever the future holds, the Soviet Union will never be the same again. The process of economic transformation may slow down, but even if it were to stop the previous system could not simply be restored as if nothing had happened. If the Soviet Union is to meet the everyday demands of its citizens as well as the needs of its security, there is no alternative to the present policies. This is the point on which Mr Gorbachev's economic advisers constantly insist. That there should be opposition to the changes is hardly surprising; a transformation of the economic climate always provokes domestic opposition, whether in Brazil, Britain, Poland or the Soviet Union. In the phrase of a Soviet economist, Soviet industry has to get out of a warm bath and stand under a cold shower. It is easy to believe Soviet spokesmen who say that no one opposes *perestroika* for others, but few admit that it need apply to their own activity. The process, however, is launched; it is being pressed forward purposefully and with courage, and the resolute style of the new Soviet leadership gives it a better chance of success than any other attempt in the last 40 years to modernise economic and social conditions in the Soviet Union.

Western leaders have recognised that if concentration on the internal problems of the Soviet Union leads the Soviet government to be more eager for relaxation of tension and a reduction of armaments, then this process must be beneficial to the West. So also must moves towards the economic and political reform of the Soviet Union in so far as they serve to improve the life of Soviet people and lead the Soviet Union to play a more constructive role in the solution of world problems. It would be foolish to suppose that the Soviet Union will forsake the pursuit of its own interests; but there have been, even outside the sphere of arms control and disarmament, some encouraging signs of change in the way in which the Soviet Union sees its role in the community of nations. The change in the Soviet attitude to United Nations peacekeeping, demonstrated by the decision to begin paying contributions and to include past arrears of payment, is noteworthy, as was the Soviet role in facilitating the election of a new and more generally acceptable Director General of UNESCO.

One could, of course, imagine some much less favourable future perspectives. It is always possible that a new arms control measure of an importance comparable to the US-Soviet treaty abolishing land based intermediate-range and shorter-range nuclear missiles in Europe might, like the SALT II treaty eight years earlier, fail to obtain the majority in the US Senate necessary to ratify it. Such a setback would almost certainly deal a severe blow both to hopes for further East-West disarmament measures and to the cause of *perestroika* and *glasnost* in the Soviet Union. Opposition in the Soviet party and government establishment to Mr Gorbachev's reforms might be strengthened by riots or disturbances in Eastern European countries, or even in the Soviet Union itself, which resulted from price increases, lay-offs or shortages caused by the introduction of reform measures. Finally, there is always the possibility of some unfortunate blunder which by its timing and its power to shock can blight the new growth of confidence and trust or sour the milder atmosphere of US-Soviet relations. The shooting down of the KAL-007 airliner was an example of just such a lamentable incident and of its repercussions.

To achieve a breakthrough in East-West relations is a matter of statesmanship, the convergence of interests, a coincidence of domestic political concerns and a measure of luck. A sustained period of improved relations is even more difficult to achieve. The most notable feature of US-Soviet, and to a less degree British-Soviet relations over the course of their history has been the tendency for them to oscillate between extremes. Warm cordiality succeeds to a period of icy disdain, to be followed by a renewed enthusiasm for closer relations. With the US the alternation is even more marked; periods of intimacy between two continent-sized superpowers, each claiming a revolutionary background, give place to bouts of reciprocal execration. If the future is to be more stable and predictable, ways of reducing these swings of the pendulum will have to be found.

Implications for Europe

Even at a time of optimism such as the present, the course of prudence suggests two main alternative courses for the next few years. The less favourable of the two presupposes that the policy of pursuing arms control agreements between the US and the Soviet Union falls victim to the winds of domestic politics, that the progress of economic and political reform in the Soviet Union and Eastern Europe stumbles and falters, and that stagnation resumes its sway in the Soviet Union, which, however, retains its great military strength. A mood of frustration in the US over the difficulty of managing East-West relations surrounds the early years of the new President. Meanwhile, the souring of the US-Soviet relationship causes concern in Western Europe and imposes further strain on the transatlantic relationship, probably leading to further and more determined efforts to create a distinct European defence identity.

The more favourable alternative would be the outcome which would enable the leaders of East and West alike to claim that their policies had been vindicated. Arms control agreements would make possible a reduction of the costs of defence, thus spurring on the process of reform in the Soviet Union but causing some problems in the defence-oriented sectors of Western economies. Intra-European contacts would develop and the relationship of the smaller states of Eastern Europe with the Community and with individual Western countries would become increasingly easy and relaxed. The successes of a revitalised Soviet economy would begin once again to make it appear an attractive model for developing countries, and the competition between the two systems would be in the provision of ploughshares rather than the manufacture of swords.

Eastern and Western leaders alike proclaim their desire that the conflict between their societies should never take military form and should be fought out as a conflict of ideas. In this there is no doubt that they express the will of the vast majority of the people they lead. But there is equally no doubt that the conflict of ideas will not rapidly or easily be resolved and, therefore, that the process of reduction of nuclear arsenals and even of conventional armaments will not of itself lead to a tranquil world. It will certainly reduce the tension existing between the groupings of East and West and will create an atmosphere of co-operation which will help in the resolution of conflicts arising both in Europe and elsewhere in the world. But the two alternative hypotheses for the future outlined above will have one characteristic in common; they will enhance the role of Europe. The process of integration of the twelve members of the European Community is to attain a new qualitative level in the 1990s. The Community is already seen by the nations of Comecon, the economic groupings of East European states, as a partner with which they have to negotiate. Its economic power in relation to that of the Comecon nations and even of the United States and Japan is becoming constantly more evident. In this economic and political context the nations of Western Europe will be increasingly concerned about their security arrangements. This concern is likely to grow if tension is relaxed between the superpowers and political pressure gains strength in America for the withdrawal of US troops from Europe, or whether renewed hostility between the US and the Soviet Union encourages Europeans once again to attempt to play a moderating or mediating role between the superpowers. In either case West Europeans will have an interest, for economic as well as political reasons, in developing their own relationships with their Soviet neighbour on the continent of Europe, rather than allowing those relationships to depend principally on the degree of hostility or co-operation between the United States and the Soviet Union. As the allies of the Soviet Union in Eastern Europe become more differentiated by their styles of economic management as well as by their diverse and rich cultural traditions, they will become increasingly interesting partners for their West European neighbours.

Much depends on domestic developments in the two halves of Europe. The political alignments of the postwar periods seem to have been shifting during the 1980s. On the one hand, many West European countries have been governed by a new brand of conservatism. On the other hand, the 1980s have witnessed the emergence of new social movements, particularly peace movements, in Western Europe whose concerns cannot be fitted neatly into the traditional antagonism of capitalism versus socialism. These developments, among others, do offer the possibility of shifting the terrain of domestic debate away from the somewhat ossified argument about state versus market between left and right towards a distinctively European discussion about the prospects for peace and the nature of democratic politics.

A parallel process has been taking place in Eastern Europe. Starting with Solidarity in Poland, autonomous social movements, on the margins of legality, informal networks of clubs and circles, sometimes under the umbrella or in co-operation with the Churches, have made their appearance in countries like Hungary,

Poland, Czechoslovakia, and East Germany. Again, these groups are much more concerned with issues like conscientious objection, military-patriotic education in schools, East-West dialogue, pollution and so on, than with the perennial debate about how the economy is organised. They represent the possibility of re-vitalising what Gramsci, following Hegel, described as 'civil society'. They argue that the existence of social relationships that are autonomous and independent of the state, described by George Konrad and Vaclav Havel as 'anti-politics', is a necessary condition for democratisation in their societies. Gorbachev's reform from above, they say, has to be complemented by reform from below, if it is to succeed.

Much will depend in the future on how far these developments continue. A dialogue, at the level of the citizen, as well as a dialogue between governments, could help to spread and popularise these new issues and to increase understanding of different societies. Even in a new and healthier situation, in which European states increasingly co-operate with each other, the conflict of ideas that originally gave rise to the Cold War will continue to have a powerful influence on the structure of relations between the European nations of East and West. But as new concerns and controversies grow in importance and indeed change the dominant political assumptions in both East and West the earlier ideological preoccupations of the Cold War may come to seem less important as a determining factor in international relations. (The background from which these potential changes are coming is set out in Chapter 4 in the section on Europe and the superpowers.)

We may be living at a hopeful time in Soviet-American relations, and in relations between the various nations in Europe, and this hope has a Christian dimension for it is hope for a world even now in the process of transformation. But what distinguishes Christian hope from secular is that the incentive to go on working for a transformation of international relations would still be present even if times were unpropitious. This chapter has sketched out some hopeful futures. But even if everything went sour, active Christian hope would remain. Moreover, it is as much part of the duty of the Christian church, in good times, to warn people against facile optimism as it is part of its duty in grim times to keep people from despair and cynicism.

Summary

There can be little doubt that we are living at a time of considerable movement between East and West and within both sides of this historic divide. We cannot be certain of the outcome. It is possible that setbacks will drive us back into mistrust and a return to the Cold War. At the other extreme the movement for change could get so out of control that it threatens our security through the breakdown of established patterns of international relationships. If these futures are to be avoided and the changes taking place turned to the advantage of peace and greater openness, the process of adjusting the political, economic and military arrangements will have to be managed with care and control. The Christian gospel urges us to engage in this task as part of our concern to give substance in the present to the hope offered to the world in Jesus Christ.

8
Meanwhile Deterrence

The Character of Nuclear Weapons

The issues of peace, disarmament and nuclear weapons were last debated by the General Synod of the Church of England on 10th February 1983.[1] The debate was, in its way, a landmark and has been much commended. Nevertheless a count has shown that, even on the most generous basis, less than 10 per cent of the words spoken that day could be said to come under the heading either of theology or of Christian ethics. There is more to be said on both these scores; and the world has moved on as well. Deterrence is worth re-visiting . . .

A useful starting point is the providence of God. Christians believe that God created the universe; and if that is so, then it is incontrovertible that he made it in such a way that the energies locked up in the atomic nucleus could in certain circumstances be unleashed for good or ill. Christians believe that God created humankind; and if that is so, then beyond doubt he endowed us with inventive brains which would in due course learn to decode and utilise in various ways (many as yet unrealised) these nuclear potentials. Christians believe that God knows what is *in* people: their propensity to sin and the misuse of all his gifts. Hence it must be within God's foreknowledge that men and women have chosen to make nuclear *weapons* and proceeded with the minimum of delay to use them.

The Christian doctrine of God's providence implies that he is in control and that therefore we must have faith. The question is faith in what? Given the history, it cannot be that God will necessarily intervene to prevent nuclear weapons being used, for this he has already declined to do. The Christian doctrine of a loving God, who works through our free choices, mistakes and failings, makes it impossible to believe that if such a war came God would 'overrule', so that in some way the end result would turn out to be what God had willed in the first place. Nor are there any grounds for Christian confidence that if a nation were to disarm then God would protect it from its enemies—assuming that it had any. Men and women have to take responsibility for their own actions and decisions and to stand by the results. This is the way God's providence *works*. So, as Bishop John Austin Baker has said:

> when we have done our best, in the light of what God has shown us both of our own nature and of his grace and moral will, then the result will help forward his kingdom. But to find out what the 'best' is that we have to do, we must look beyond the doctrine of providence.[2]

If a blind trust in providence is one, too-hopeful, way of opting out of the nuclear dilemma, a second, more pessimistic and indeed deeply disturbing one is to be found in the concept of divine punishment. This is relevant to the nuclear debate not least because in the Bible God's punishments are sometimes depicted in the form of heat, blast and chemical strikes visited upon whole communities. Luke (9.54) records the instance of a Samaritan village refusing to receive Jesus, because his face was 'set toward Jerusalem'. James and John, incensed, asked:

> Lord, do you want us to bid fire come down from heaven and consume them?

It seems a curious story. Did James and John think that he might call down a strike? Even President Reagan at his most folksy would hardly have mooted it for failure of hospitality. Jesus, not surprisingly, rebuked them and they went on to another village. A footnote in the Revised Standard Version tells us that other ancient authorities add:

> and he said, 'you do not know what manner of spirit you are of, for the Son of Man came not to destroy men's lives but to save them'.

Even more puzzling is the instruction given by Jesus himself to the 70 evangelists (Luke 10.10):

> Whenever you enter a town and they do not receive you . . . I tell you, it shall be more tolerable on that day for Sodom than for that town.

Sodom, it will be recalled, was rained upon by fire and brimstone from the Lord out of heaven and totally destroyed (Genesis 19.24). In this connection it seems grotesquely disproportionate. Matthew (11.24) promises a similar fate specifically for Capernaum, but that is for lack of repentance and is deferred till Judgement Day. And this, perhaps, provides a clue. It may be that these exchanges belong, not to the context of planning for the next night's rest, but to the realm of *apocalypse*. (See Chapter 2 on the interpretation of apocalyptic themes in the New Testament.)

Thus all three synoptic gospels record a passage in which Jesus, speaking to a select body of disciples, forecasts the coming of the Son of Man on clouds in power and glory. This is to be preceded by a period of dire troubles (wars, famines and earthquakes) and then —the sun and moon are darkened, stars fall and 'the power of the heavens will be shaken' (Matthew 24.29, Mark 13.25, Luke 21.26). Peter writes of the day of the Lord's coming in similar terms:

> and then the heavens will pass away with a loud noise, the elements will be dissolved with fire, and the earth and the works that are upon it will be burned up.
>
> (2 Peter 3.10)

Evidently these ideas represent a strong and pervasive strand in the original tradition. The events so described were hoped for, and expected within the lifetimes of the original disciples-or so it seems. This did not happen. What *did* happen in the years AD40–70 were famines, the Jewish revolt of AD66, a guerilla war against the local garrison, the reduction of the country by a large army under Vespasian and the siege of Jerusalem by his son Titus. When the city fell the walls were broken down, the Temple burned and the inhabitants dispersed. The Jews' last attempt to win independence had ended in catastrophe and they had to wait almost 1900 years for another. This was very bad. But when all allowance is made for oriental hyperbole and the use of metaphor it is hard to see the real events of AD70 bearing any of the hallmarks of the promised coming of the Lord. The texts quoted above may even have been written *after* AD70. We are compelled, if we are to take them seriously, to regard them as warnings of events which could still lie in the future. What connection can they have with issues of peace and war in our time?

If we have understood the doctrine of God's providence correctly there is no guarantee that a major nuclear war will not take place. If it did, and particularly if the theory of 'nuclear winter' proved to be well founded, then much of the apocalyptic imagery of the gospels could pass, with due allowance for poetic licence, as factual description. It is possible that some of the same things seem to have happened, at the time of the destruction of the dinosaurs 65 million years ago, as a result of meteorite impact. The same catastrophe could now be brought about by human deeds. If so, then there would be no incongruity in regarding what had happened as, in some sense, God's punishment for sin. What is quite impermissible is to regard any such denouement as inevitable—because pre-ordained—or, still worse, as a sign to be hoped for in the sense of Jesus' injunction to the disciples in Luke 21.28:

> Now when these things begin to take place, look up and raise your heads, because your redemption is drawing near.

It is absurdly anthropocentric, not to say blasphemous, to equate the outcome of a nuclear war on earth, however dire, with the type of cosmic catastrophe prefigured by the evangelists. This latter has much more in common with the 'heat death' of the universe foreseen by cosmologists as lying billions of years in the future. It belongs to the *end of time*: to times and seasons that are not for us to know. As Chapter 2 makes clear, what matters for us is to retain the hope both of a renewed earth and of the coming of the City of God: but not to look for them in our own time and, assuredly, not through the mechanism of a nuclear war.

What then is morally significant about nuclear weapons? They produce blast and heat, which are only too familiar. Used in large numbers (and the numbers available are very large indeed—literally *myriads*—tens of thousands) they could produce dust and smoke in such quantities that they *might*, by blotting out the sun, produce long-term lethal damage to the environment. Of course, whole areas of the earth have been depopulated before by fire and sword by 'barbarians', by military attrition (the Thirty Years War in Germany), by man-made desertification (the Sahara), and by 'natural' causes: movement of the ice-caps, the Black Death. But the scale of the disaster, both in duration and extent, would probably be unprecedented. Nuclear weapons also produce ionising radiation, both in the form of immediate neutron flux and of residual radiation, some of which decays only over a period of decades, if not centuries. The latter may be spread through the atmosphere to cover huge areas. There is something eerie about radiation sickness. It may kill fast or slowly or maim for life. It can affect children in the womb. Possibly, it could damage generations unbegotten at the time.[3] In the past, of course, more people have always tended to die in war from sickness than by the sword. People hideously maimed from the First World War are still alive. Children in the womb are killed by terrorists' bullets. And as for human reproduction this has to take its chance amidst radiation of cosmic, geological or therapeutic origin, and power stations out of control. It is easy to overlook the appalling character of 'conventional' wars. The war of 1865–1870 in Paraguay is said to have obliterated nine out of every ten male adults throughout the country. In the Second World War the firestorms in Dresden and Hamburg and the bombing of Tokyo were as lethal as the two atomic bombs. Conventional weapons are now far more destructive than they were then. And any large-scale fighting in Europe would be likely to cause damage to nuclear power stations (even if inadvertent) leading to tens, if not hundreds of Chernobyls.

Above all what is perhaps most significantly novel about the evils of nuclear war is not the *types* of damage to be apprehended, but their scale, duration and suddenness, set against the complex and vulnerable nature of modern industrial society (none of which has a unique moral dimension) and the fact that for the first time in history all this could be set in train by the actions of a tiny handful of individuals. In today's terms perhaps only the war cabinets of the five nuclear weapons states have the powers of decision-making which could induce a major nuclear war catastrophe. It is in this fact that the moral implications of nuclear war chiefly reside.

Weapons and Morality

One merit of this analysis is that it turns attention away from nuclear weapons as such. Much supposedly ethical discussion goes wrong at this point. It is not weaponry that causes wars or determines their scope and lethality. The Second World War, in its pre-nuclear phase, encompassed 50 mega-deaths. One of the bloodiest conflicts since then, between the Hindus and Muslims at the partition of British India, was fought with the most primitive of weapons. What, therefore, is evil is not weaponry as such (not even nuclear weapons). The evil (or good) resides in the actions of governments, that is of human beings.

The heart of the Christian ethic is easy to state.

> Love your enemies
> Do good to those who hate you
> Bless those who curse you
> Pray for those who abuse you.
>
> (Luke 6.27)

> My kingship is not of this world.
> If my kingship were of this world then my servants
> would fight that I might not be handed over to the Jews.
> But my kingship is not from the world.
>
> (John 18.36)

> For we are not contending against flesh and blood but against the principalities, against the powers, against the world rulers of this present darkness, against the spiritual hosts of wickedness in the heavenly places. Therefore take the whole armour of God, that you may be able to withstand in the evil day and having done all to stand . . . and take the helmet of salvation and the sword of the spirit, which is the word of God.
>
> (Eph. 6.10–17)

One can see in all this one clear and intelligible strand of teaching which cannot be wished away as a pacifist overlay put on by the synoptists, because it runs back through the whole tradition and equally clearly forward into the early Church. Christ and the Christians see themselves as at war with spiritual enemies, Satan and his legions. Healing miracles and exorcisms are an important part of their activities and an important proof of their claims. Their weapons are the weapons of the spirit, for only so can evil be defeated. They disapprove not only of bloodshed but of hatred. Everyone who hates his brother is a murderer. Christians are under an obligation to love their enemies, respond to curses with prayer and to violence with gentleness, for in so doing they exercise a greater power. No one, in the face of this record, can deny the validity of an individual Christian vocation to non-violence. But states cannot live in this way, nor can they die sacrificially, for to do so would be to deny their whole function and nature, at least in the world as we know it.

The New Testament does not have a great deal to say about the role and vocation of states. It does, however, recognise their obvious functions of restraining evil doers and of raising taxes (Romans 13.3–6—see Chapter 3 for an interpretation of these verses). If the state is to execute the wrath of God on the wrong-doer within, then *a fortiori* the state needs the means to defend itself against enemies without. As a matter of hard fact every nation on earth has equipped and does so equip itself. The means are manifold, ranging from diplomatic apparatus at one extreme to weapons of war at the other. It is always better to settle disputes, if one can, by persuasion and agreement than by fighting. A half-way house, less evil in principle than fighting but more so than negotiation is the deliberate use of the weapon of fear. If this is used to coerce a weaker nation it becomes blackmail and is rightly condemned as an abuse of power. If it is used to withstand coercion or to prevent fighting then it becomes deterrence, and is obviously a better thing than waging war. Thus it was no more than commonsense when the General Synod, at the end of its debate on 10th February 1983, affirmed by the unusual margin of 387 votes to 49 (with 29 abstaining):

> that it is the duty of Her Majesty's Government and her allies to maintain adequate forces to guard against nuclear blackmail and to deter nuclear and non-nuclear aggressors.[4]

So far so good. But just as the internal powers of the state have to be curtailed and abridged in accordance with the precepts of Natural Justice, so have the external powers of the state to be constrained in accordance with concepts of Natural Law. There is a range of possible forms of deterrence, from the threat of civilian resistance, to the threat of conventional defence, through to the threat of nuclear retaliation. Two considerations need to be taken into account whatever the form of deterrence. First, the system must be dependable in the sense of durable, stable and effective. The threat has to be credible. Secondly, as far as possible, no action must be countenanced that is or has consequences in conflict with the Christian conscience. We take these in turn.

Arrangements for deterrence need to be durable. The vision of an effective Anti-Ballistic Missile (ABM) system rendering nuclear weapons both 'impotent and obsolete', as in certain expositions (including the first) of the American President's Strategic Defence Initiative (SDI); and *a fortiori* the dreams of their total abolition, which surfaced in some versions of the discussions at Reykjavik, seem oddly disconnected from the realities either of technology or of *realpolitik*. By the turn of the century things may look different, and there will be time enough to re-assess. For the present SDI smacks too much of technical hubris. The belief that technology can offer a way out of dependence on nuclear deterrence is ill-founded, for that will require political and not technical change. At the same time it may undermine current stability.

Arrangements for deterrence need to be as stable as possible, whether in peace, in crisis or in war. The criterion for peacetime is simply stated; that is, to carry the conviction, to any conceivable opponent, that the price of war would be so high that in no circumstances must he run the risk of being dragged, drifted, cajoled or tempted into one. Some practical implications will be mentioned later in terms of forces and supporting structures. On the other hand, the arrangements for deterrence should not themselves contribute to hostility and exacerbate the underlying causes of conflict. In choosing the appropriate form of deterrence we need to balance the risks associated with these two aspects; the risk that a given level of military threat generates mutual fear and mistrust, against the risk that a lower level of threat might not be sufficient to inhibit an enemy attack.

The political setting is equally important. In Europe, whether or not nuclear weapons have contributed to keeping the peace during the last 40 years, what surely has done is the political, social and economic self-confidence and cohesion in both East and West, coupled with the clear recognition of the territorial status quo. Of course, there have been violent upheavals in Eastern Europe. While it may be desirable to work for the elimination of the two alliance systems in the very long term, this process can only accompany the relaxation of enmities; it cannot lead it.

In crisis there is need of arrangements which create the minimum incentive to go to war, whether to seize an advantage or to forestall disaster, and the greatest inducement to refrain. This means that the assessment of issues and the taking of decisions by the top political authorities must be done only with due deliberation and in the fullest possible understanding by each side of what the other is thinking and doing. The institutional machinery for these purposes deserves as much thought and preparation as the weaponry and its logistics.

In war these arrangements need to be even more efficient and their survival is of the highest priority. It should be the aim, as far as possible, both to control and to limit the use of force even in the direst of emergencies, such as a pre-emptive attack.

It is equally important to recognise that the deterrent system itself needs to be operationally effective. The difficulty with nuclear weapons is that they do not exist simply as a context within which the normal transactions of diplomacy can be conducted. The notion of 'existential deterrence'—that nuclear weapons deter war by their very existence, irrespective of any prospect of their use—is a form of bluff. But is that good enough? If deterrence is to be credible, sailors, soldiers and airmen would, if the worst came to the worst, have to obey the command to fire. Thus they have to be trained and mentally conditioned. Their job is a very demanding one and sometimes dangerous. They cannot be made parties to an elaborate charade. So there has to be a concept for use. The danger is that in developing a concept of use, the use of nuclear weapons becomes thinkable, thus blurring the distinction between weapons of deterrence and weapons of war.

The foregoing suggestions all fall under the heading of 'dependability', being intended to ensure, as far as possible, that deterrence works: this being the duty that the General Synod enjoins. We turn now to the second criterion: that no action must be countenanced that is in conflict with the moral conscience. A convenient starting point is the theory of the Just War, which has its roots in Augustine, was developed by Aquinas and given shape by more recent authors such as Vitoria and Suarez. It has no one definitive expression[5] but among the more important elements are always two:

First, *Jus ad Bellum*, the requirement that war should have a just cause. For all practical purposes this is now taken to mean that, while a war of aggression or aggrandisement is wrong, it is morally licit to go to war in self-defence, for the protection of one's land and people. For a war to be just there has also to be a reasonable chance of winning. Since in a nuclear war of any magnitude everyone understands that there could be no winners in the traditional sense, and since even a conventional war in Europe would risk the destruction at least of Germany as a civilised society, by winning is now meant bringing any war to an end as quickly, and with as little loss of life, as possible. If defence could not achieve this then, as matters stand today, there would be no justification for fighting at all and it were far better to surrender. This is not a question of being better red than dead. That slogan is quite meaningless. After a major war, any major war in Europe, the very fabric of social life—schools, hospitals, cities, water and food supplies and structure of government would have been wrecked to a degree where one could attach no meaning to the phrase 'defence of Western values'. The differences between East and West Germany today pale into insignificance by comparison. While there is life there is at least the hope of liberty. It is, of course, with precisely this end in view, of stopping any aggression dead in its tracks, that Western policies for nuclear use have been configured. Not that a just intention is enough. One might have miscalculated the outcome. Many think that escalation (on the metaphor of the moving staircase) is much more probable. But we are talking at the moment only of Just Cause.

The second ingredient of Just War is *Jus in bello*, the requirement that war should be justly conducted. And in this consideration there are two key notions: proportionality and discrimination. *Proportionality* requires that the evil to be inflicted both in the war as a whole, and in particular operations, should not exceed the evil that would be suffered without it. Here one cannot avoid taking a view on likelihood. To take one example. If the result of a nuclear first use by the West was to stop a major Russian incursion stone dead, then the strategy in question would have proved itself to be both rational (in that it produced its intended effect) and moral (to the extent that it would have saved many lives and preserved our freedoms). If, contrariwise, escalation occurred and went to the limit, it would have been impossible to conceive of a more irrational and immoral action in the whole of human history. The difficulty is, of course, that the morality of any action has to be judged by the participants in advance. A measured action by the West might be met by a wildly intemperate Russian response. The virtue of prudence is to allow for this. *Discrimination* goes further. It requires that even in a proportional war, the innocent are not harmed directly and intentionally. Here two clarifications are in order. The first is that innocence does not mean absence of martial intent. Soldiers may be unwilling conscripts. Civilians may be just as closely implicated in the war effort as the military or, in the case of political leaders, even more so. Innocent means doing no harm, not contributing: children, old people, the sick, the handicapped, the mentally ill. These play no part in the conduct of the war and the war must not be conducted against them. But what of unknowing damage? This introduces the second distinction, of 'double effect'. It holds that innocent casualties are justified if they occur as the unintended result of attacks upon legitimate targets, and are not disproportionate. It might, for example, be possible to devise a limited damage plan which, while eschewing counter-population strikes and concentrating primarily on military and related targets particularly an adversary's conventional forces and their supporting infrastructure, was still prepared not to rule out damage levels sufficient to convince an aggressor that the costs of any aggression amply outweighed the benefits.[6] Whether such criteria govern any real targeting concepts is, of course, hotly debated.

Many believe that if NATO used nuclear weapons to try and stem a conventional Russian attack (never mind how improbable this setting seems for it is the normative one) then the likelihood of escalation is substantial. Indeed the possibility of leading to a strategic nuclear war has always formed part of the deterrent concept in the NATO doctrine of flexible response.[7] If this occurred then the actions that led up to it would be difficult to justify under the criteria for the Just War of discrimination and proportionality. The General Synod expressed the clear view that, for this reason, even a small-scale first use of nuclear weapons could never be morally justified.[8]

It cannot be proved, but there seems good reason to think that it is misgivings of this kind coupled with the paradoxical nature of a policy that seeks to prevent a nuclear war by threatening, in certain circumstances, to initiate one, that has persuaded NATO governments and military authorities that the nuclear component in the Western defensive system ought to be downgraded and de-emphasised: that nuclear weapons should be replaced with conventional ones as far as technology makes this possible and stability permits. Advanced conventional weapons are not inherently less destructive, but they produce no fall-out and above all they avoid crossing the nuclear rubicon, with all the potentiality for escalation that this implies. So while this would by no means be a cheap policy, and could be seen as a provocative one because effective attacks on, for example, enemy airfields would not have to await nuclear 'release', nevertheless most people of goodwill have welcomed it.

The General Synod wanted to go further; wanted Britain and her allies 'publicly to forswear the first use of nuclear weapons in any form'.[9] Such a step could be very important psychologically, creating a climate in which the likelihood of conflict is diminished. But as a measure of arms control, this suggestion is insufficient. It could not, by definition, be verified. No one could be held to it. To the extent that it was believed it could diminish the stability of deterrence. A 'no first use' regime has been in place since 1925 in the field of chemical weapons, yet stockpiles have persisted on the argument of deterrence of like by like. It would be better to regard this proposal as aiming at a desirable evolution of NATO policy, by the adjustment of the balance between nuclear and conventional forces, to the point where first use of nuclear weapons should neither be relied upon nor needed.

An alternative approach, more relevant to the creation of mutual confidence, is that implied by the General Synod's further assertion: 'that the tactics and strategies of this country and her NATO allies should be seen to be unmistakably defensive'.[10] The crucial word is *seen*. NATO itself well knows, and its leaders have repeatedly affirmed that none of its weapons would ever be used save in reply to an attack. Nevertheless there are aspects of NATO's military preparations that the Russians profess to see as needlessly provocative, the 'forward-basing' of American nuclear systems being an obvious example. By the same token there are aspects of Warsaw Pact deployments which are seen, rightly or wrongly, by the West as threatening: most notably the preponderance of Russian armoured forces. Recognising this problem, the May 1987 meeting of Warsaw Pact leaders in Berlin addressed the point precisely. It spoke of establishing 'minimum force levels that could be defensive only . . . within a structure and such a style that they would be in a position to repel an attack'. The Warsaw Pact offered talks, at expert level, in which these ideas could be mutually explored.[11] It would be foolish if not gravely immoral not to take up the offer.

How Many Weapons?

The General Synod's final call was for the 'decrease of nuclear arsenals throughout the world'.[12] This echoed the judgement, given by Pope John Paul II in the previous year, that deterrence 'might still be judged morally acceptable' only if it were 'a step on the way towards a progressive disarmament'.[13] Indeed it seems likely that all right-minded people, let alone Christians, would want to see nuclear weapons minimised in the sense of being as few in number and as cheap as is consistent with doing the job for which their owners acquire them: to deter war between possessors and to extend an 'umbrella' over friends. It is common ground that the present and planned inventories far exceed these minima. But the arguments in favour of less provision can easily be mis-stated. One of the favourite reasons is to free resources for better uses, typically the relief of human needs. But as Barrie Paskins has pointed out this is not a necessary consequence.[14] It would depend on whether reductions in nuclear weapons were part of a political process of reconciliation or whether nuclear weapons were replaced by conventional weapons. Clearly it is also important to press for mutual reductions in conventional weapons.

It is not self-evident that fewer or cheaper nuclear weapons will in some way be less dangerous. So far as war by misperception or miscalculation is concerned, this argument does not hold. Sir Arthur Hockaday has shown that the conditions for mutual stability in deterrence may be quite narrow.[15] As the number of systems come down the danger of moving into a zone of (at least theoretical) instability increases. Where the argument has force is in the realm of technical malfunction, human error or simple accident. A reduction in numbers of weapons would lead to some reduction of risk, albeit much less than in direct proportion. Related to this is the consideration that if the world's stockpile contained a total yield of only hundreds of megatons the likelihood of triggering a climatic catastrophe might be very significantly reduced.

Some would argue that reductions in the numbers of weapons are less important than calling a halt to their 'sophistication'. For example it is held that the introduction of Multiple Independently-targeted Re-entry Vehicles (MIRV), by increasing the dividend from a 'first strike', has decreased the stability of the system. The same is often said of more improvements in accuracy and reductions in time of flight. But the opposite applies to measures which make delivery systems less vulnerable (mobile basing, and the less ambitious versions of the SDI) or which improve the survivability of Command, Control, Communication and Intelligence. So distinctions are needed. Reductions need to be designed in such a way as to diminish any incentive to strike first. A Comprehensive Test Ban (CTB), for example, is normally seen as a useful way to control the technical innovation which lies at the heart of the arms race. On the other hand it might prove a bad bargain if it resulted in dangerous obsolescence or doubts as to whether systems actually still worked.

The most important argument in favour of reducing both the numbers and the technical advance of nuclear weapons is political rather than technical or military. If we are serious in wanting to bring about a reconciliation between East and West, it is very difficult to make progress as long as we are pointing nuclear weapons at each other. If we believe that it is right to threaten the use of nuclear weapons then this also implies a profound mistrust of the other side, a belief that the other side would commit evil of such proportion as to justify the use of nuclear weapons. Reductions of nuclear weapons could help to reduce that mistrust and provide the conditions for further agreements.

After years of apparently barren effort, a way to make progress has suddenly opened up. It consists of the progressive elimination of *types* of nuclear weapon system. The nuclear mortar (Davy Crockett) was an obvious nonsense and soon abolished. It seems that nuclear land-mines (Atomic Demolition Munitions—ADM) and surface to air anti-aircraft missiles (Nike Hercules) have also been scrapped. Meanwhile the total number of nuclear warheads for battlefield nuclear systems has been reduced from 7,000 to some 4,400, all by unilateral action on the NATO side. This is a good start.

Next for attention have been Intermediate Nuclear Forces (INF); by which is meant land-based nuclear ballistic and cruise missiles with ranges between 300 and 3,000 miles. The INF Treaty signed in Washington in December 1987 provided for the total abolition, over a three-year period, of all such missiles and their warheads, other than the French. The numbers of missiles to be destroyed are admittedly modest in relation to the total of nuclear systems. But the significance of the Treaty is much more far reaching. For the first time since the Second World War an agreement is in place, between America and Russia, which caters for the reduction of nuclear weapons as opposed to limiting their increase. The agreement is asymmetrical, in the sense that the Russians are destroying 3,000 warheads against the Americans' 800. And the procedures for verification break totally new ground; notably with the agreement that Soviet and American officials are to inspect each other's nuclear facilities on the spot and, where appropriate, on challenge, over a period of some 13 years. In all these ways, and more if hopes of building up mutual confidence are fulfilled, this Treaty could serve as a model for still better arms control agreements in the future.

The INF Treaty, while supported by all the NATO governments, has occasioned some alarm and chagrin in some quarters in Western Europe. It has, to a large degree, been arranged over the heads of the Europeans, some of whom feel shut out. The

West Germans, in particular, resent the situation where remaining land-based nuclear systems, on both sides in Europe, can only strike targets on German soil. They see a case for abolishing these systems also: indeed it would have been more logical to begin with them. The short range of these weapons means that their military usefulness is small, and their potential for instability ('use them or lose them') quite large. However the NATO agreement, referred to above, to reduce the number of warheads on battlefield nuclear weapons went hand in hand with plans to 'modernise' the delivery systems in the shape of shells, rockets and air-delivered munitions of greater range than their existing counterparts. While these plans may be perfectly logical, particularly if they lead to a still further reduction in warhead numbers, they are obviously more difficult to defend particularly in a post-INF climate. And this difficulty is compounded by proposals that the Americans should make 'compensatory adjustments' to offset the removal of the INF: say by stationing aircraft armed with air-launched Cruise missiles in the UK or by earmarking submarines carrying sea-launched Cruise missiles for the NATO European Command. These weapons are very similar to the ground-launched Cruise missiles being abolished under the INF agreement so that any such substitution would look like a contradiction of the spirit (though certainly not the letter) of the Treaty. What matters above all is to maintain the unity of the North Atlantic Alliance. It would therefore be wise to focus, as the next step, on reductions in conventional forces and chemical weapons. The removal of INF, which provide a tangible means of striking Russian targets with American missiles from European soil, is already seen as a dilution of the American nuclear guarantee. The presence in Europe of more than 300,000 American service men and women and their families is by far the strongest remaining token of American involvement. Some American troop withdrawals may well take place in any case for budgetary reasons. It is clearly desirable to situate these withdrawals within a framework of mutual Soviet and United States withdrawal. Hence the next step in nuclear disarmament should be sought elsewhere.

It is in strategic systems that over-provision is most flagrant.

The combined inventories of the USA and the USSR amount to some 20,000 warheads with a total yield of some 10,000 megatons. The declared intention of both sides is to achieve 50 per cent reductions in the number of warheads, at least as a first step. If this could be brought about it would be precisely in line with the papal criterion—a step on the way toward a progressive disarmament—that is 'balanced, simultaneous and internationally controlled'. This very promising approach is stalled on the issue of Anti-Ballistic Missile Defence, and is crying out for compromise.

Meanwhile two other long standing arms control negotiations could now be given a fresh impetus. Both sides are ready, in principle, to conclude a treaty eliminating chemical weapons. The difficulties of verification are acute because a chemical shell or bomb looks no different from any other. The concept of mutual inspection of facilities, on the spot and on challenge, which figure so largely in the INF Treaty, did, in fact, originate from the chemical weapons negotiations. If they work well the whole problem will look quite different, and rapid progress may be expected.

A more intractable problem is that posed by conventional forces. There is need, at one and the same time: to move in the direction of much less reliance on first use of nuclear weapons; to come to terms with possible American troop withdrawals; and yet to make do with allocations of manpower and money no larger than, and almost certainly smaller than, have been available in recent years. It is tempting, but too optimistic, to assume that these problems could be resolved by French agreement to re-integrate within the NATO structure (or into a European 'pillar' of the NATO structure), perhaps accompanied by Spain. That failing, there remains in logic only one way to reconcile these conflicting objectives: by means of negotiated conventional arms reductions both within NATO and as between NATO and the Warsaw Pact. Talks to this end (the so-called Mutual and Balanced Force Reduction Exercise—MBFR) have been in progress in Vienna for the last 15 years with negligible product, and it is easy to doubt that the successor discussions, 'from the Atlantic to the Urals', will have any greater success. Nevertheless both in this area and in the parallel Stockholm negotiations on

Confidence Building Measures (CBM) there are signs of a fresh political impetus and of much greater readiness to accept measures of mutual reassurance. The Warsaw Pact declaration previously quoted[11] recognised the need for whichever side is ahead in any particular category of forces to scale them down, and proposed the withdrawal of the most dangerous forms of offensive weapons from the immediate zone of contact. It may well be, therefore, that the new Conventional Stability Talks (CST) will also issue in workable arms control agreements. It is, of course, the fear of Warsaw Pact superiority in chemical and conventional offensive capabilities that has provided the rationale for NATO battlefield nuclear weapons and the concept of 'first use'. There is therefore no reason, in principle, why some measure of reduction in battlefield nuclear weapons should not accompany the CST process.

In the longer term, rather than total abolition of Strategic Systems or, alternatively, of all Inter-Continental Ballistic Missiles, both of which figured in the Reykjavik post-mortem, a much safer alternative might consist of a limited number of mobile nuclear ballistic missile delivery systems, including submarine-based systems, on either side with no Anti-Ballistic Missile systems other than those allowed by the 1972 Anti-Ballistic Missile (ABM) Treaty.

Meanwhile it is clearly important to preserve the stability of the international system, recognising that this could be threatened as much by inflexibility and unwillingness to change. But changes take time. It took 15 years for the (potentially catastrophic) doctrine of 'massive retaliation' to be supplanted by the far more credible concept of 'flexible response'. The withering away of the (morally questionable) nuclear first use component could well take even longer. Fears and differing perceptions have to be massaged away. Individual nations may wish to contribute to this process by independent steps towards disarmament which could help to break the log jam of multi-national negotiations and contribute to a wider détente. Gorbachev's unilateral test moratorium and the steps recently taken by Holland, Belgium, Spain and Greece to give up certain nuclear tasks are good examples. Unilateral Soviet troop withdrawals from Central

Europe would contribute substantially to the success of conventional negotiations. However, it is clearly important that all such steps should be taken on the basis of co-operation and consultation both with partners and opponents.

So long as the necessity for deterrence, whether conventional or nuclear, remains, there is a balance to be struck and a price to be paid. To deter is to dissuade by fear. The balance is between on the one hand making war so unspeakably nasty that no one could be tempted into it and on the other so terrifying people by deterrent preparations that they act irrationally. The price is that, if you are saddled with possession of weapons as destructive as the nuclear bomb, you need distrust of any enemy to justify your having them; by implication you must believe that your opponent is evil enough to deserve having them used upon him. Like other high levels of militarism this sours the international scene, but to a degree without precedent. So, to a unique degree there is a moral obligation to hold the balance steady and force down the price. We cannot see an end to the necessity for some kind of deterrence. It may persist as long as the risk of war itself, whilst humankind remains too clever and not good enough.[17]

Chapter 7 explored the changes now taking place in Soviet-American relations. We now look for a continuing improvement in these relations, which will express itself in further arms reductions as suggested above. But as Chapter 1 made clear, Shalom and Pax exist in tension with one another so long as life on earth continues. The vision of a transformed world in which coercion will have no place tussles with the world we actually have in which coercion, in one form or another, helps to keep war at bay. The task of the Church is not only to encourage the transformation of the world in the light of the vision of Shalom but to urge realism in order to ensure that the essential benefits of Pax are not sacrificed to an unrealistic romanticism or a sentimental view of human affairs. For some of us this means that deterrence of a minimal kind, with a continuing nuclear component, will be an essential feature of the relationships between the superpowers for the foreseeable future. Others of us, whilst accepting the necessity of deterrence, believe that we should divest ourselves of the nuclear element in a way that looks for, but is not dependent upon, a reciprocal response.

Summary

The theory of deterrence and the strategies which have been developed to give it effect are designed to prevent war breaking out between East and West. There is a lively debate among Christians and others about the moral defensibility both of the theory and the strategy. All are agreed, however, that both theory and strategy need to be held within the boundaries of moral principle. The use of the tradition of the Just War theory is critical to such moral accountability.

In the present climate of greater openness in East-West relations and the pursuit of new arms agreements, it is clear that progress could be made at many levels in the reduction in the level of threat from both nuclear and conventional arms. The changing political climate is bound to affect the way we see our need for defensive systems. Again, as we have seen elsewhere in this report, the opportunities need to be both grasped and managed if they are to be turned to the advantage of peace between East and West.

Footnotes

[1] *The Church and the Bomb*. The General Synod Debate, February 1983. CIO Publishing, 1983.

[2] John Austin Baker, *Theology and Nuclear Weapons*, Kings Theological Review. Vol. VI, No. I, Spring 1983, p.1.

[3] *Hiroshima and Nagasaki: the physical, medical and social effects of the atomic bombings*. Hutchinson, 1983, p.115.

[4] *Op. cit.*, in footnote 1, p.67.

[5] See for example: Richard Harries, *Christianity and War in the Nuclear Age*. Mowbray, 1986. Chapters 6–9.

[6] *Morality and the Bomb*, David Fisher. Croom Helm, 1984, p.90.

[7] White Paper 1970 on the Security of the Federal Republic of Germany. English Language version, pp.27-28.

[8] *Op. cit.*, p.68.

[9] *Loc. cit.*

[10] *Op. cit.*, p.67.

[11] Soviet News. 3rd June 1983.

[12] *Op. cit.*, p.68.

[13] Message of His Holiness Pope John Paul II on the occasion of the Second Special Session of the United Nations General Assembly Devoted to Disarmament. New York. 11th June 1982, p.7.

[14] Barrie Paskins. Deep cuts are morally imperative. In *Ethics and Nuclear Deterrence*. Geoffrey Goodwin ed. Croom Helm, 1982, p.112.

[15] *In Defence of Deterrence*, Arthur Hockaday. *Op. cit.* in footnote 14, p.75 *et. seq*.

[16] *Loc cit.* in footnote 13.

[17] *The Profession of Arms*, General Sir John Hackett. Sidgewick and Jackson, 1983, p.214.

9
Détente and Reconciliation

'Détente' means the relaxation of tension, and is a necessary preliminary to the enormously complex process of making peace. But certain tensions in life are unavoidable and may indeed be fruitful. One need not be a fully-fledged Hegelian or Darwinian to accept the truth of the Heraclitan epigram, 'strife is the father of all things', and recognise the necessary contribution which conflict has made to the development of human experience. Christianity may, like Marxism, promise an eschatological peace, but both Christians and Marxists see peace as a goal for which we have to strive. Strife is part of the task set before us, whether by 'history' or by God. True peace, Shalom, can only come about through the triumph of a just order, and it is over the nature of that just order and the best way to achieve it that political conflicts, whether domestic or international, inevitably arise. It is by definition impossible to achieve peace through abandoning our own perception of justice and ceasing to strive for it, for an order we perceive as unjust can provide no true peace.

Détente, therefore, may provide Pax, the absence of war: a situation in which necessary and inevitable conflict can continue but is confined within agreed and acceptable limits and pursued by non-violent and legitimate means. But Shalom can be prepared for only by a far deeper and far-reaching process: that described by Christians as 'Reconciliation'. It is this that must be maintained as the goal of our efforts. Détente, Pax, necessarily imperfect, is only a means to this ultimate end. Thus the theological distinction, which we discussed in Chapter 1 between Shalom and Pax helps us understand the relationship of détente and reconciliation in the process of making peace.

Conflicts arise because the perceptions we hold of 'justice' and 'order' are *sub specie aeternitatis*, parochial and incomplete. That is why they are in conflict. But we cannot transcend our historical limitations and play God. We have to work with the tools and conceptions with which we were born. Even if we were to accept a total moral relativism—something which is for Christians doubtfully legitimate—we have a duty to implement our concepts of justice and order within our own societies and, arguably, assist those who share our values in other societies. Further, the position of the moral relativist becomes more difficult to sustain as improvement in communications links the world into a single global society in which separate cultures are brought into immediate contact and competition with one another. The creation of such a society may indeed ultimately produce a consensus on value systems and distributive justice of the kind for which we are striving, but unless all social and economic development within it is then somehow frozen indefinitely, further conflicts of different kinds are still bound to occur. Kant's depiction of perpetual peace as a graveyard must always be born in mind: total peace comes only with the end of growth and change.

It is in this context that the concept of Christian hope, which we discussed in Chapter 2, is of such supreme importance. For some the realisation that the surge and ebb of conflict in history is never ceasing, that calm seas will always sooner or later be stirred up by deep ocean swells and storms, that there is on earth no safe haven where we can rest and that no amount of expertise, technological or rational, can create one, is cause only for despair. It was the destruction of such nineteenth-century optimism by the wars and tyrannies of the twentieth century that led some liberals to embrace the false dawn of communism and others to the kind of nihilism to which H. G. Wells was reduced at the end of his life: 'Mind at the End of its Tether.' But for the Christian this realisation is nothing new. We have never been led to expect in this life anything else. Our hope lies elsewhere. Yet this does not mean that we can or should abstract ourselves from the world in which we live: the commandment to love our neighbour imposes on us a duty of citizenship, of responsible membership of the *polis*. That means that we have to partake in *politics* and accept the necessary conflicts and antagonisms—many of them with our fellow Christians—which this inevitably entails.

Much of what follows is therefore cast in political terms which are not specifically Christian, except insofar as they deal with the defence and survival of a society whose values have been shaped by Christianity and whose structure enables Christianity, as God has given us to understand it, to persist. Its mode is prudential. But even in the secular realm of prudence, Christians can contribute one essential insight. At the base of Christian politics lies the commandment to love, not just our neighbours, but our enemies as well. As has been often pointed out, this does not mean that we have to *like* either of them. But it does imply that we may have to accept the existence of enemies, whether we have deserved them or not. The duty of love is one of empathy: of entering into the minds of our adversaries, understanding why they hold their values, why they act in the fashion they do, why they mistrust and dislike us so much. Even when they commit acts apparently of monstrous evil we have a duty to understand how they came to behave in such a way. Such understanding will not necessarily relax tensions. It may, and possibly should, sharpen them. But what Christians should never do is to view a purely secular adversary as the embodiment of evil, however evil his acts may appear to us and however just we feel our cause to be. Our secular duty to defend our *polis* must never be dressed up as a holy war.

What in the light of all this are we to say of the conflict between the Western World and the Soviet Union, that Cold War which has dominated international politics throughout the second half of our century? First we have to accept that there is a *real* conflict; not one caused by misunderstanding and misperception which can be eliminated by better understanding and rational discourse. It is a conflict in three areas: ideology; political culture; and national power.

First there is the problem of ideology caused by the postulates of Soviet Marx-Leninism. We are not talking here of Marxism as such. We considered that more fully in Chapter 2. The insights which Marx and his successors developed into the nature of social development, the tools they devised for the analysis of political problems, all have been absorbed into and enriched the intellectual bloodstream of the West. Most Western Marxism is quite compatible with the kind of democratic pluralism which we are concerned to preserve. But the Marxism which Lenin and his successors fastened upon the Soviet Union is of a peculiar kind. In the first place it postulates a party *apparat* whose unique insight into the historical process gives it a total right to control the thinking of the entire population; exercising a dictatorship of belief on behalf of a notional 'proletariat' backed by the full resources of state power. Party and state are inseparable and interdependent. In the second place it promulgates the millennial belief, abandoned by most Western Marxists, in the inevitable triumph of socialism and the coming of a communist earthly paradise, free from all strife, through the operation of the objective forces of history. Finally it assumes, as a necessary part of that doctrine, the implacable hostility of the bourgeois-imperialist societies which surround it. Their ultimate dissolution is certain, but they are constantly plotting the pre-emptive destruction of the Soviet Union, the focus of the revolutionary forces which will one day overthrow them. It would be a grave mistake to believe that simply by assuming a non-threatening military posture the West could change these Soviet perceptions: our hostility is seen as an intrinsic and ineluctable part of the historical structure, and can end only when the capitalist system itself is overthrown. Only then, in the teaching of the Soviet Marx-Leninist pundits, can there be true *mir*, universal peace.

Secondly there is the nature of the Soviet political system. This is to be distinguished from the Marx-Leninist ideology which legitimises it, for so much is an inheritance from the Czarist regime which it replaced and can be explained only in terms, not of Marxist theory but of Russian culture and history. The xenophobia, the omnipresent secret police, the oppression of political dissidence, the brutality with which the government treats its subjects, the suppression of minorities, the vast, lethargic and corrupt bureaucracy, all this is a heritage from the past. It must be remembered that throughout the nineteenth century the Russian Empire was loathed and feared by Western liberals and Marxists alike as a bastion of reactionary despotism. Alliance with her in the First World War caused as much liberal heart-searching as it did in the Second; indeed, considerably more. It is thus not just an ideology but a culture to which Western concepts of 'human rights' are very largely alien, except among a handful of courageous and Western-oriented intellectuals. Western individualism indeed is regarded as profoundly divisive and corrupting in a society where historic roots lie deep in peasant collectivism.

Finally there is the sheer power the Soviet Union derives from its size, its population, its economic self-sufficiency, and its capacity to channel its resources into military strength through the degree of social control it exercises over the peoples which compose it. This is a secular, long-term problem unrelated to the nature of regime itself. Paradoxically, a liberalisation of the regime could result in a growth in the economic strength of the Soviet Union and enable her to exercise yet greater power. Russia shares with all states unendowed with defensible frontiers the desire to control its weaker neighbours, for fear lest if she does not do so, a stronger adversary will: hence her determination to dominate Eastern Europe—a determination unlikely to be affected by any change in her internal regime. She is also likely to continue the search for influence, if not outright control, over her southern neighbours, Iran and Afghanistan, and to counter Chinese power by building up a friendly Vietnam on China's southern border. She may become a yet more formidable power in the Pacific. Irrespective of their ideology the Russians are constrained by their geographical situation to partake in the process of international power-politics, and in so doing to come into conflict with interests which her neighbours, and the West in general, are legitimately concerned to sustain and defend.

This growth of Soviet power might create a serious danger of incremental imperialism. With all previous empires in history, the appetite for expansion tended to increase with eating. On the other hand, growing self-confidence might reduce the paranoia of Soviet leadership and make them more relaxed in their dealings with the West.

The Soviets would claim, indeed, that all their apparent expansion is reactive and defensive, and it is important for us to understand why the Soviet Union views its neighbours with alarm. To the East lies the enormous, still largely untapped power of China, with her openly revisionist demands on Soviet territory. Beyond her southern borders, and constantly threatening to overlap them, there is the menace of Islamic fundamentalism, with all the attraction this holds out for the Moslem populations of Central Asia. As for the West, the quarter from which Russia has been invaded three times in the past two centuries, it is not only Marx-Leninist ideologues who see its pluralistic-liberal societies as alien and threatening. The atomistic individualism inherent in Western doctrines of 'human rights' has always been repugnant to peoples whose cultures are deeply rooted in the concept of the community. The dynamic of free-enterprise capitalism—the only truly revolutionary force in the nineteenth and twentieth centuries—threatens traditional values in the Soviet Union as well as the precarious political structures established there since the Revolution. And the continuing ability of the West—which must be taken as including Japan—to outpace the Soviet Union in every branch of technological innovation, save those (such as space-technology) regarded as so essential as to need an exceptional concentration of resources, reinforces the inferiority complex from which the Russians have suffered *vis-à-vis* the West since the time of Peter the Great. In trying to persuade the Soviet peoples that they are under threat, their leaders are pushing at an open door.

In all these areas, ideological, cultural and political, some degree of conflict with the West is unavoidable. The problem is not how to avoid, but how to defuse and contain it: how to demythologise the Cold War and create a relationship with the Soviet Union no worse, if no better, than that which obtains among the states of the West, where rivalry is taken for granted but peacefully pursued, competition for influence or economic advantage does not impede friendly relations, and areas of co-operation are explored and gradually extended: above all where our military forces are not seen as reciprocally threatening. Within the horizons of our limited human perceptions and responsibilities, it would be unrealistic to set ourselves for the time being any more ambitious goals for détente.

All our efforts at détente and reconciliation, however modest, would be in vain if the Soviet leadership remained frozen in a position of ideological hostility which made them regard international politics as a zero-sum game and see peace as resulting only from the ultimate triumph of socialism. Fortunately Lenin, a master of the art of translating political necessity into ideological dogma, provided a way of escape through the doctrine of 'peaceful co-existence'. Bourgeois capitalism, he taught at the end of his life, had to be accepted as a fact of life and cohabited with; at least until the correlation of forces changed to the advantage of the Soviet Union so decisively that the time was clearly ripe to overthrow it. How far this alarming corollary of the doctrine of peaceful co-existence is still taken seriously by Soviet élites it is impossible to say, but its very existence makes it difficult for the West to enter into agreements with the Soviet Union with any great degree of confidence in their long-term intentions.

But Soviet ideology is in a state of flux. No ideology can be understood if we view it simply as an intellectual concept. Its content may be derived from insight, reason, or revelation, but its political acceptability and influence depends, as Marx himself observed, on the social environment from which it arises and to which it gives expression. For a people in a state of post-revolutionary turmoil and threatened on all sides by powerful enemies, the harsh *dirigisme* of Marx-Leninism, in spite of all its inequities and the atrocities to which it led at the hands of Stalin, made sense to intelligent Soviet citizens as a necessary instrument of social control. It was acceptable if only as an alternative to anarchy and defeat.

But gradually, painfully, conditions did improve. Improvement created growing consumer expectations particularly among those classes whose higher education, especially in technology, was a necessary part of the process of economic development. Literacy, urbanisation and modernisation have today created a class within the Soviet Union increasingly impatient of the rigid Byzantine orthodoxy of the prevalent ideology and its persistent failure to match promise with performance. All too clearly it is not capitalism that is failing; it is socialism itself. And how can that be explained?

It would be naive to attribute the current turmoil within the

Soviet Union to the initiative of one remarkable man, and perverse to see it as a tactic to disarm the West. It would be equally naive to expect any sudden mass conversion. Hard-line Marx-Leninists will continue to occupy key positions in the Soviet administration for years to come. Attitudes of hostility and suspicion, practices of deception and subversion legitimised since the Revolution and general long before that may take at least a generation to disappear, if indeed they ever do. But there are grounds not only for Christian but for secular hope that a growing proportion of the Soviet élites are coming to realise that their country cannot flourish in isolation, that the bourgeois West with all it has to offer is a necessary partner in Soviet prosperity and that attempts to undermine it politically and exploit the crises of capitalism are highly counter-productive for the Soviet Union itself. All this is being reflected in Soviet writings today.[1] With such people serious dialogue is possible, and such dialogue is in itself a form of détente.

The ideology of Marx-Leninism may thus gradually cease to constitute the impenetrable obstacle to East-West reconciliation which it has been for the past 70 years. Marxism in the Soviet Union may evolve as it has in Western Europe, or as indeed has Christianity itself: abandoning its eschatological certainties, accepting that the dialectic is a continuing, perhaps a permanent, process and that revolutions are no more than historical incidents from which no earthly millennium can be expected. But we in our turn would have to accept that the Marxist diagnosis may often be correct; that conflicts between classes or indeed between races over perceptions of a just order may reach a point where they can only be resolved by violence. If Marx-Leninists must abandon their expectations of a revolutionary millennium, many people in the West must accept that the millennium has not in fact arrived; that we have not ourselves established an order so just that all we have to do is to preserve and defend it. In a serious dialogue with well-informed Soviet critics we would have quite as much to learn about the inadequacies of our own social system as we would have to teach them about theirs.

What of the second obstacle to East-West reconciliation—the fundamentally collectivist nature of Soviet society and its apparent lack of concern for Western concepts of 'human rights'? Here much depends, again, on the evolution of the Soviet system. But more serious for our purposes than Soviet oppression of minorities and suppression of political dissidence is Soviet censorship—yet another heritage from the Russian past. The problem is not just that the Soviet peoples are not permitted to express views at variance with those prescribed by the Party. It is that they are denied access to sources of information which could enable them to formulate such views. In dialogue with Soviet citizens, including highly intelligent professional colleagues, one rapidly comes up against a blank wall of ignorance, particularly about the past; ignorance reinforced at official levels by breath-taking mendacity. The ideological myth which legitimises the Soviet system depends for its credibility on keeping the Soviet peoples themselves ignorant both about the past and about the present, and hedging them about with a bodyguard of lies.

One of the most encouraging aspects of the present Soviet regime is the extent to which this very system is now under attack; not so much because of any moral objections as because it makes impossible either efficient government or thriving economy. Some degree of secrecy and deception may be necessary in all societies, but when elevated to the level of a mandatory principle it frustrates the whole purpose of government. The more this becomes realised throughout the Soviet Union and the more *glasnost* penetrates the conduct of international as well as of domestic politics, the easier it will become to deal with her as we deal with other friendly states, and cease to see her as an adversary against whom we can never entirely let down our guard.

As for 'human rights', this is a problem which does not affect the Soviet Union alone. If we were to cultivate friendly relations only with those nations whose record in this respect measured up to the standards of the liberal West, we could drastically reduce the Foreign Office vote. The double standards so often applied to human rights abuses in the Soviet Union and to those in many Third World countries friendly to the West are unacceptable to the Christian conscience. The Soviet record in this respect is particularly repugnant, partly because of the sheer scale of human-rights abuses, and partly because certain minorities which suffer from them, such as the Poles and the Jews, have powerful voices in the West. But it must be repeated that this is a problem of culture rather than ideology. There is no reason to suppose that Soviet suppression of minority peoples and groups is always opposed by the Russian people. Certainly we have seen nothing in the past 30 years to parallel the anti-Jewish pogroms which the Czarist regime carried out, with the enthusiastic support of the local population, at the end of the last century. To use 'human rights' as a weapon in political confrontation, linking it with political and economic concessions, is bound to be widely perceived in the Soviet Union as a crude form of blackmail, and can only make the position of oppressed minorities very much worse. Nevertheless as was argued in Chapter 5, a constant and frank statement of our views, reminding the Soviet leadership of the gap between their ideological pretensions and solemn undertakings on the one hand, and the political realities of the situation on the other, is a course from which we have no need to shrink; so long as we do not object if, perceiving the gap between promise and performance in our own societies, they choose to retaliate in kind.

For no more than Marx-Leninism can the liberal ideology of human rights be understood outside its social context. The Marxists are right: although deeply rooted in Christian values, the concept of 'human rights' as generally understood in the West dates from the 'Enlightenment' of the eighteenth century and is associated with the ascendancy of prosperous middle classes whose success depends on their being given full scope for their individuality. It flourishes primarily in societies whose stage of economic development both permits and requires it. In most societies throughout history the needs of the community have been given precedence over the rights of the individual, as they still are in the Soviet Union today. Individuality is no virtue in tribal or peasant communities. But we are today witnessing in the Soviet Union a process of *embourgeoisement*—one perhaps delayed for half a century by the Bolshevik revolution and its aftermath—which may create precisely those circumstances which encourage respect for human rights as the West understands them. We must guard, however, against any assumption of linear development whereby a 'backward' Soviet Union will 'catch up' with a more mature West. Cultural diversity will remain a historically-determined condition, and we must be prepared to co-exist with a neighbour whose value-system may continue to be, in many fundamental respects, very different from our own.

Finally we face the problem of Soviet power in the international arena—a problem whose nature may be changed by internal developments in the Soviet system, but which will certainly not disappear. This affects us most immediately in Eastern Europe. There Russian determination to preserve a sphere of influence from which all potentially hostile elements are excluded has up to now conflicted with the desire of those peoples to control their own destinies. The leaders of the Soviet Union still seem to believe that the security of their country depends on the maintenance in Eastern Europe of a political order which is perceived by the mass of Poles, Czechs and Hungarians as being patently 'unjust', although Soviet reformers have recently talked about learning from experiments in socialism and some have even questioned the correctness of the Soviet intervention in Czechoslovakia in 1968. A relaxation of East-West military and, even more, ideological tensions may induce the Soviet Union to modify the rigour of its control, but it could still feel impelled to retain a dominant presence in the area; not only through fear of a West whose renewed hostility can never be totally discounted and whose cultural attractiveness to their satellites is unlikely to diminish, but because successful national self-assertion in those regions might have serious repercussions within the Soviet Union itself. The harsh dilemma remains for us, that détente with the Soviet Union might have in the short run to be purchased at the expense of the peoples of Eastern Europe, and some in the West find this too high a price to pay.

Yet it is hard to see how those peoples can possibly *benefit* from a continuation of East-West tensions or from promises of 'liberation' in which no one any longer believes. Arguably it is the peoples of Eastern Europe who have suffered most from the Cold War, and from its relaxation they have most to gain. Even if they still have to work out their political destinies within a framework of Soviet power, rendering unto an alien Caesar the things that are Caesar's, they could only benefit from the normalisation of relations between the Soviet Union and the Western world, and the freer contacts between the two halves of Europe which might be expected to follow. So long as the Soviet Union retains its political domination over Eastern Europe there can be no question of reconciliation—Shalom. But it may be a necessary condition of détente—Pax. Relaxation in relationships between the West and the Soviet Union may help in allowing greater flexibility between the Soviet Union and Eastern Europe.

The West must be equally philosophical about the presence of Soviet power elsewhere in the world. The Russians will be as reluctant to see the Gulf become a Western lake as is the West to see it fall under Soviet domination, and will strive for influence over their neighbour, Iran. Withdrawing from Afghanistan is a difficult and painful process. They will continue to cultivate clients and pursue their interests in the Middle East. Their conflict with China, the historical roots of which go far deeper than those of their conflict with the West, will determine their policies in the Far East, and in the Third World nationalist Marxist regimes will continue to look to them for a support which Soviet leaders may well see as being in their national interest, as well as morally justifiable, to give. However far-reaching the process of détente, in short, the Soviet Union will still act like a State. However good their overall relations, the West will not always find Soviet activities acceptable and may need to act firmly to counter them.

But State relationships can be co-operative as well as conflictual, and co-operation and consultation can mitigate conflict even if they cannot eliminate it. Anglo-French relations in the Middle East continued to be sulphurous for half a century after the entente of 1904, and there have been long periods when Anglo-American relations in that region were no better. But gradually co-operation has won out over conflict, even if conflict has never quite disappeared. Conflict and conflict-resolution is the very stuff of diplomacy, and it already operates between the West and the Soviet Union to a far greater degree than is commonly realised. In a world in which East-West détente had effectively been achieved, the Soviet Union and the West would not approach every issue on the assumption that for its opponent this was simply a move in a long-term game aimed at their own ultimate destruction. Conflicts might still be unavoidable and bitter, but they would no longer be lethal; and both sides would see an increasing interest in maintaining a framework to ensure that they were not. This framework might not in the short run involve 'disarmament' as such; but it would certainly call for far-reaching and mutually-agreed measures, whether explicit or implicit, of arms control some of which involved substantial reductions in weapons and troops.

It must also be accepted that such a 'normalisation' of relations will demand a radical transformation of some Western attitudes as well. There are those for whom settled hostility to the Soviet Union has become so intrinsic a part of their world picture that nothing is likely to change it. This may arise from a temperamental need to have an enemy, a devil figure in whom all the evils of the world are incarnate—an attitude deplorably prevalent among certain fundamentalist sects in the United States, for whom the Soviet Union is quite literally the embodiment of evil. It may be fuelled by the experiences, whether direct or inherent, of those who have suffered at the hands of the Soviet regime, particularly Poles, Jews, and members of the dispossessed ruling classes. Others still see the Soviet Union as the focus of an undifferentiated 'Communism' which threatens their values and their lifestyles; while for some the disappearance of such an adversary would leave them bereft of an occupation. Such Manichean attitudes exist and will remain powerful within the Soviet Union as well as in the West. There will still be influential figures on both sides who will put the worst construction on all their adversary's actions, base all their thinking on worst-case analysis and whom nothing will convince that they are not confronting a foe implacably bent on their own destruction.

Such attitudes are usually impervious both to evidence and to argument, and so long as they are prevalent on the other side we would be unwise to ignore the warnings of the pessimists on our own. Yet the more we learn about one another, the less convincing these stereotype caricatures become. Whatever Marx-Leninist ideologues and their adversaries may profess, no amount of censorship can conceal from Western scholars the confusion and incompetence of the Soviet regime and the diversity of views being expressed as to what should be done about it. Free circulation of information within the Soviet Union about the outside world would destroy the image projected to the Soviet peoples by their leaders, of a capitalist-imperialist West dedicated to the destruction of socialism in general and the Soviet experiment in particular. With such openness and dissemination of information, each society might come to see the other as the mass of confused human beings that we are, wrestling with the difficulties presented to us by our history and more concerned with solving our own problems than with eliminating our adversaries: not to be trusted, perhaps, but more to be pitied than feared. At least we would understand one another better. Such understanding, as we have seen, does not necessarily engender either mutual confidence or mutual affection. But without it there can be neither détente in the short run nor reconciliation in the long.

Summary

The Christian understanding of peace as both Shalom and Pax resonates with the political tasks of establishing détente in the midst of a world of divided interests, ideologies and power and the search for reconciliation between power blocs which have such a long history of suspicion and mistrust of each other. There can be no reconciliation unless first there is détente just as there can be no Shalom unless there is Pax.

Furthermore we have seen both in Christian thought and in the experience of history that conflicts are not necessarily bad. They are part of human experience and, if acknowledged and managed, can provide the context in which we are able to develop and change.

It is possible that we are living at a moment of significant change in East-West relations. If such change is to be turned to the cause of peace it will have to be managed through a careful process of détente. It is to the management of East-West relations that we now turn our attention.

Footnote

[1] A good summary is to be found in Stephen Shenfield, *The Nuclear Predicament: Explorations in Soviet Ideology*. Chatham House Papers. RIIA and Routledge & Kegan Paul, London & New York, 1987.

10
The Management of East-West Relations

Keeping Communications Open

Sydney Smith, Canon of St Pauls at the beginning of the nineteenth century and a famous wit, was walking with a friend down a narrow London street. Above their heads, two women leaning out of the windows of houses on opposite sides of the street were hurling abuse at each other. Smith remarked drily to his friend, 'Alas, they will never agree, for they argue from different premises.'

The same remark might be made of the long and often acrimonious argument which has set East and West at odds for several decades. Applied to questions, discussed in the last chapter, of ideology, political organisation, economic structure or attitudes to human rights, the remark might be apt. But there are some matters to which for some years both East and West have manifestly come to believe that it does not apply. The avoidance of nuclear war and the value of reducing the numbers of deployed nuclear weapons are premises which the two sides have acknowledged that they have in common, and this common ground, relatively recently acquired, has contributed to the evolution of a relationship of greater trust. The creation of such a relationship offers the best hope that new arms control agreements can be achieved which will have a good prospect of enduring.

Given the profound differences of outlook and philosophy, of historical experience and of self-perception which set the two superpowers apart, the difficulties of developing a relationship which will be resistant to the recurrent shocks which are inevitable in international affairs must not be underestimated. Whether the euphoria created by the Reagan-Gorbachev summit meeting in December 1987 is sustained or fades as a consequence of some fresh disagreement, it is possible to find much encouragement for the future merely by looking back at the distance we have already travelled in the right direction.

East-West summit meetings are no longer a rarity. In the 1980s it would be surprising if in any year there were to be no more than one meeting between the General Secretary of the Communist Party of the Soviet Union and the leader of one of the major Western nations. Such meetings, now almost a regular feature of the diplomatic calendar, would have been difficult to imagine in the years of the Berlin blockade and the twilight period of Stalin's rule. The fact that no summit meeting occurred for the ten years between 1945 and 1955 was an indication of the sterility of East-West diplomacy in those years. When a meeting of Soviet and Western leaders took place in 1955, the extreme public optimism about its outcome was natural enough; the preceding years had seen little genuine high-level communication between East and West and such exchanges as had taken place, when not merely vituperative, had been largely a dialogue of the deaf. Whatever crises and difficulties have punctuated the development of East-West relations over the 30 years since those first high-level encounters, communication between East and West has, in its range, quality and detail, improved out of all recognition. Even if genuine amity has yet to replace suspicion, each side has acquired a much subtler and more sophisticated understanding of the other.

The four difficult decades which we have survived since the end of the Second World War have not enabled us to eliminate crises in East-West relations, or even to reduce greatly the frequency of their occurrence. They have at least given us a chance to learn how to manage crises when they do occur. It is especially at a time of crisis that rapid, reliable and authoritative communication is required, as was vividly demonstrated during the Cuban missile crisis of 1962. That crisis has been the subject of many studies; not surprisingly, since by common consent it was the moment in the post-1945 era in which the world seemed to come closest to war, the moment of which Khrushchev said in retrospect, 'There was a smell of burning in the air.' This was, however, the moment at which the arts of crisis management were most skilfully employed. Diplomatic channels were by no means the only important mode of communication between the adversaries; signals indicating strength and resolution, but also readiness to compromise, were sent by means of changes in military and naval dispositions, conversations between unofficial Russian and American emissaries, direct messages between the leaders and, most importantly, a television broadcast by President Kenedy which was in reality addressed to an overseas audience which included the Russian leaders as much as to the American people. It has been said that from start to finish this crisis turned on communication, especially the communication of attitudes and capabilities between President Kennedy and Mr Khrushchev.

But if successful communication made possible the solution of the crisis, failure of communication probably helped to start it. It seems likely that Khrushchev, at his first meeting with Kennedy in Vienna, judged that a man young enough to be his son, and one who had made a misjudgement over the failed invasion of Cuba (the Bay of Pigs), would lack the firmness and tenacity to react effectively to a new dramatic move from the Soviet side. More frequent meetings and a more regular schedule of meetings, such as is the practice today, might have averted that misjudgement.

Managing Disagreements

The lessons of this alarming episode have evidently been studied with as much care in Moscow as they have been in the United States. 'Hot lines' have been installed, and constantly improved, between Moscow and Washington (and between Moscow and some other Western capitals). Methods of communicating intentions and of managing crises have become more refined. Nevertheless, however efficient the fire brigade may become, it is preferable not to be obliged to call it out. It is much better to prevent an international crisis from arising than to attempt to manage it when it has already reached a dangerous stage and when the stakes have been raised. Governments in East and West have an obvious interest in receiving advance warning of an impending crisis; yet despite the range and diversity of intelligence resources, the mechanisms of diplomacy, the consultative structures of the

United Nations and the availability of a variety of unofficial channels of communication, the record of governments in East and West in foreseeing international crises and, more particularly, in forewarning each other of a crisis which is likely to upset their relations, has been at best an uneven one. Whatever advance notice the Soviet government may have been disposed to give to Western governments of its intentions in Afghanistan or in Poland is likely to have been short, and US actions have clearly been a complete surprise to the Soviet Union on more than one occasion. Moreover, serious tensions are often created suddenly by unforeseen events such as a military coup or an assassination, or perhaps by the unexpected revelation of embarrassing information which one side or the other had hoped to keep secret (for example, through the defection of a key official from the Soviet Union or the leakage of a document in the West). These crises have to be managed when they occur; to make this easier, it has been suggested (by Dr Coral Bell in a paper on Communication Strategies)[1] that some form of crisis-warning or crisis-avoidance machinery could be set up to forestall crises before they reach an acute stage. Such machinery, it has been suggested, could be a joint enterprise of the superpowers or possibly of the five permanent members of the Security Council. This idea has some attractions and deserves some further study. It is, however, unlikely to be well received by smaller nations who would feel that their own interests would not be adequately considered, and it would in any case require a greater and more sustained degree of superpower harmony than has existed in the recent past. It is nevertheless an idea which could serve the purpose of managing disagreement rather than allowing it to become inflamed.

The policy of peaceful co-existence between states with differing social systems, proclaimed by the Soviet Union, was quite consistent with this idea. President Brezhnev attached importance to the US-Soviet Agreement on the Prevention of Nuclear War signed in 1973, and his successors seem to have regarded the principles underlying that agreement as having continuing validity. When in the years following 1979 East-West relations became embittered, it was not always remembered that some years earlier the two superpowers had signed a formal undertaking in which they recorded that an objective of their policies was to remove the danger of nuclear war and of the use of nuclear weapons. They also agreed that they would act in such a manner as to prevent the development of situations capable of causing a dangerous exacerbation of their relations, to avoid military confrontations and to exclude the outbreak of nuclear war between the two of them as well as between either one of them and other countries, and they bound themselves to enter into urgent consultation with each other to avert the risk of nuclear war if relations between them or between either of them and other countries appeared to involve such a risk. This agreement, in the negotiation of which Mr Brezhnev took a close interest, was accepted by the US as:

> a reflection of the belief that control of arms presupposed restraint in international conduct and that coexistence between the superpowers would ultimately depend on adherence to standards of behaviour by which they would learn not to threaten each other's vital interests.

These words of Dr Kissinger seem just as relevant today as they did 15 years ago.

In the course of those 15 years, the United States took the view that the Soviet Union's failure to exercise restraint in their involvement in other areas of the world (e.g. the Middle East and Angola) justified them in assigning to this agreement a lesser degree of significance than the Soviet leaders evidently did. The Soviet leadership did not restrain its criticism of American actions which, in its view, violated the spirit of the 1973 Agreement; but it did not move to revoke it. The signing of the Agreement was itself evidence of the recognition by the superpowers of a substratum of common interest between them, but it was inevitably fragile. By reason of the breadth of the obligations it imposed, it depended more than other agreements on the maintenance of the trust of each party in the sincere upholding of it by the other. The agreement, moreover, came at a time when the process of détente was running into difficulties. By 1973, it was becoming clear that arms control would not of itself promote détente; détente would be needed to produce the trust required for arms control. Yet the very process of arms control tended to undermine trust. Unless the concept of common security was accepted, there was a natural tendency for each side to scrutinise every arms control proposal put to it with the presumption that it was intended to gain unilateral advantage. Proposals for intrusive verification were regarded as demands for licensed espionage; rejection of such proposals was denounced as unjustifiable secretiveness. The notion of 'confidence-building measures' was seen as offering a way out of this impasse. It was hoped that this new device might help to resolve these dilemmas and give a new impulse to the conciliation of differences.

The Creation of Confidence

It was at the 1975 CSCE Conference in Helsinki that confidence-building measures were first embodied in an international agreement. They may have been modest in scope and effect, but at the time they were welcomed as a significant advance. Some even thought that they represented a new approach to arms control at a time when the traditional path towards arms reduction agreements seemed to be strewn with ever more obstacles. The weapons in the arsenals of the two superpowers could not be neatly paired off category by category, and to find acceptable balances and 'trade-offs' was a difficult task. The quest for balanced reductions raised difficult problems of the phasing and timing of reduction measures, since neither side would be likely to acquiesce in a position of inferiority, even temporary, in relation to the other. The advent of smaller, more mobile weapons made concealment easier and thus posed new problems of verification. 'National technical means' of verification (the conventional term for satellite surveillance and electronic intelligence resources) would have greater difficulties than before, it was foreseen, in providing convincing evidence of compliance. Then again, there were new worries about 'balance'. The old concerns about the East-West strategic balance were supplemented by new ones about regional European or Far Eastern balances or by balances in different categories of forces. The attempt to ensure symmetry, or to find tolerable forms of asymmetry, was one among a variety of reasons which caused the negotiation of the second US-Soviet agreement on limitation of strategic arms (SALT II) to continue for seven years before an acceptable package was devised. Even with good intentions and shared hopes of success on both sides, some were beginning to wonder whether before long super-power arms control negotiations would be doomed to sink under the weight of their own complexity.

The Helsinki Final Act, which imposed a balance of obligations relating to security, economic and human rights issues, came in the middle of the period of negotiation of SALT II when hopes of progress on the arms control agreements were flagging. Confidence-building measures were thus endowed with a certain symbolic significance which was perhaps more important than their direct military value for reassuring the participating countries. The Confidence and Security-Building Measures (CSBMs) agreed in 1986 at the Stockholm Conference built on what had been agreed ten years earlier; the scope of the measures is larger and the obligations of the parties, especially in regard to the information and facilities they are required to provide, are set out more extensively and in greater detail. Their most significant feature is that, rather than remaining voluntary as the previous more limited measure had been, the newly agreed CSBMs had the mandatory force of an international obligation. For all these reasons their political as well as their military significance was greatly enhanced. Moreover, the experience gained in the relatively short time since the new measures came into effect has been more satisfactory than under the previous less stringent measures. Arrangements for the observations at manoeuvres have improved considerably. Pictures of NATO and Warsaw Pact officers attending each other's manoeuvres have been published increasingly frequently, and put a more human face on the dour confrontation of opposing armed forces.

Despite these advances, it was unreasonable to expect confidence and security building measures such as these to do more than lay down stepping stones. They may have helped to remove apprehensions about the intrusiveness, and thus the threat to security, which the Soviet Union so long argued to be an unacceptable feature of on-site inspection teams of observers. They have probably been of value in demonstrating how such monitoring or verification arrangements might work. If so, they may have helped to clear the path to agreement on limiting or eliminating certain categories of weapon (for example, chemical weapons) where the nature of the processes of manufacture is such that no ban could be effectively monitored by 'national technical means' unsupported by some form of routine inspection or 'inspection by challenge' to investigate prima facie evidence that a treaty breach might have occurred.

This is precisely the area in which 'confidence-building' acquires its real meaning for the arms control aspect of East-West relations. Verification of compliance with agreements is one aspect of the building of confidence, but a uniquely important one. The present size of strategic arsenals represents an outlay of resources which could be put to more productive use if the level of those arsenals could be reduced and the pace of their modernisation limited by treaty. A treaty regime may, however, be robust or fragile; it is unlikely to be robust unless the parties have confidence in each other's will to observe it. The need for verification measures to be effective is now endorsed by the Soviet side as well as by the West. Indeed, the intrusiveness of some verification requirements when applied to both sides seems to have alarmed some of the custodians of Western security.

The agreement of the Soviet Union to accept far-reaching inspection arrangements for the INF Treaty signed in Washington on 8th December 1987 may in retrospect be seen as a turning point in the postwar history of arms control. Much, however, will depend on the way in which the parties to the Treaty interpret those inspection provisions. Disagreements about the fulfilment of very complicated procedures are almost inevitable and when delays occur or ambiguous responses are given in response to enquiries, suspicions are bound to arise, especially among critics of arms control agreements. There is a need for a clear and effective method for resolving disputes. Sometimes a bilateral agreement, for example, the SALT I agreement and the Anti-Ballistic Missile Treaty, may make provision for a standing consultative committee to hold regular meetings at which evidence of possible treaty breaches can be presented and discussed with the aim of establishing just what occurred and whether the occurrence was a breach of treaty obligations. Alternatively, an agreement may make provision for a regular conference of signatories to discuss matters arising from the operation of the agreement. The purpose is the same; doubts about compliance have to be discussed with frankness (and therefore preferably without immediate and detailed publicity) and they have to be resolved swiftly if the robustness of the arms control regime is to remain unimpaired. When this does not happen a source of instability is created; public concern may arise that the security afforded by the treaty regime is illusory rather than genuine and opponents of the limitations imposed by the treaty may exploit the uncertainty. On the other hand, accumulated confidence that a treaty is being observed may, together with increased sophistication of surveillance systems, make it possible greatly to reduce verification requirements. Although there was agreement between the US, the USSR and the UK in 1958 that the total cessation of nuclear weapon tests would require over 30 internationally manned control posts located over the entire globe, such a vastly expensive operation is not considered necessary today and its absence does not appear to have reduced the confidence of governments (and indeed the public) that nuclear weapons are not being tested in the atmosphere, the sea or outer space by any government which has signed the Treaty.

On the other side, doubts about adherence to treaties can set back the whole process of controlling and eventually cutting back levels of armaments. There are still unresolved uncertainties about an incident at Sverdlovsk which might, as the Russians claimed, have been a natural outbreak of anthrax, but might have been evidence of a breach of the Biological Weapons Treaty. There is still argument about whether a very large radar installation at Krasnoyarsk is or is not a violation of the Anti-Ballistic Missile Treaty of 1972. There is continuing uncertainty in the public mind about the interpretation which the US Government will decide to put upon that Treaty and about how, if at all, the Treaty will be regarded as affecting the Strategic Defence Initiative. These ambiguities and obscurities do nothing to improve the prospect for a durable arms control arrangement between East and West. It has even been suggested that a situation in which the two sides, having signed a series of arms control agreements, then fell to exchanging accusations and recriminations about real or alleged breaches of those agreements might be almost more harmful to the international atmosphere than the failure to achieve agreements.

The period since the Synod last received a report of the subjects considered by the present Working Group has witnessed changes which indicate a modest but encouraging increase in the frankness and openness of discussion between the leaders of the Soviet Union and of Western nations. It has also witnessed the beginning of a period of change in the Soviet Union, the continuation of which may have profound effects for the extension of the range and quality of contacts between East and West and for the process of arms control. Certainly, after the Washington and Moscow Summits of 1987 and 1988 the prospects for further frank discussion of differences seemed to be better than they had been for many years. Old problems were being tackled in new ways. But confidence laboriously nurtured over years by such contacts can be quickly undermined or destroyed and hope, based on precarious foundations, can equally quickly be shown to have been foolish self-deception. Progress in reconciling deeply conflicting interests in several spheres is already difficult enough; all too easily it can fall victim to a sharp disagreement over some entirely different and perhaps irrelevant matter. Some unforeseen and unforeseeable event, such as the shooting down of the KAL 007 airliner, may suddenly cause a bitter clash at the most delicate moment of a long negotiation.

Although it would be idle to suppose that one area of East–West relations could be wholly insulated from others, in a period when important arms negotiations are at issue those negotiations can and should be given priority over others. During the SALT negotiations in the 1970s, the Soviet Union did not make the US bombing of Haiphong a pretext for breaking off negotiations, nor did the US break off the talks because of Soviet involvement in Cuban intervention in Angola. However great the temptation to make a dramatic political gesture of disapproval, arms control should be the last and not the first area in which such gestures are made. Crisis management, confidence-building, persistence in negotiating agreements to limit or reduce armaments, steadfastness in upholding those agreements—all these are of great importance in gradually transforming the atmosphere in which international relations are conducted. They will contribute to that sense that the partner in an adversary relationship is dependable and predictable—even though the limits of predictability are set by changes occurring every few years in the leadership of this or that Western nation and by frequent changes in the composition of the Soviet Politburo.

All these desirable improvements in the way in which East-West relations are handled have not and in themselves cannot be expected to eradicate the disagreements which originally set East and West at loggerheads. What they can do, however, is of immeasurable importance; they can begin and strengthen a beneficial trend of which the result could be that the competition between the two systems will no longer find its expression principally in terms of military power. The declarations of the leaders of the major nations representing the two competing economic systems frequently make plain the confidence of each that his own system has the vitality, the innovative power and the ability to meet the demands of social justice which will enable his system to prevail. That was, presumably, the meaning of Mr Khrushchev's famous and much misunderstood remark addressed to his capitalist rivals, 'We will bury you' and of President Reagan's remark that the Western democracies would transcend the Soviet system. These claims and others like them have a moral as well as a political and economic content; they assert a secure confidence in the outcome of peaceful competition between the two systems. The competition exists and, unless it is reconciled by some startling transformation in one system or the other, is likely to continue. The reality of it need not be disguised or obscured; but the effort must be made to channel its course away from the endless pursuit of military superiority. Neither alliance can be expected by the other to accept an impairing of its security or to tolerate an acknowledged situation of military inferiority; but there is still no satisfactory answer to the question posed over a decade ago by Henry Kissinger about the real meaning and value which, in an age of 'overkill' can be assigned to nuclear superiority.

Recent developments in East-West relations suggest that security can be maintained at agreed lower levels of military strength. The 1987 summit meeting seemed to promise an answer to the hopes and prayers of many that such a trend had now begun, and that in parallel with that trend the two great political and economic systems, each of which claims as its supreme aim the welfare of its citizens, would increasingly pursue their competition in the arts of peace and in bettering the lot of their populations and of mankind as a whole.

Security and Co-operation in Europe

Many different lines of approach have been advocated for the management and reduction of the tensions which seem to be inherent in the East-West relationship. No single approach will suffice, and many must be pursued simultaneously. A road which suddenly has to bear a heavy overload of traffic will before long be in danger of breaking up and the experience of the past has shown that, if arms control negotiations alone have to carry the whole weight of the détente process, that process can soon become unstable and end in disillusion. Confidence building, crisis warning and crisis-avoidance machinery, better communications, consultation at all levels and shared enterprises in diplomacy, science, commerce and culture all have a contribution to make but none will on its own be sufficient.

This gives the Helsinki Final Act its real significance; it is about the building of confidence and the creation of trust not just by governments and diplomats but by businessmen, musicians, athletes, tourists, civic delegations, writers—by all whose professional interests or private pursuits help to build bridges between East and West. The three parts or 'baskets' of this Agreement on Security and Co-operation in Europe deal with the encouragement of all such links as well as with security in the purely military sense; and equal weight is given to all the principles set out in the Agreement. It can be seen as a message of hope and encouragement addressed by the governments of the 35 signatory countries to all their citizens, and it is one to which all Christians can and should respond.

'The development of mutual understanding' is an aspiration frequently mentioned in speeches on East-West relations as something for which governments should strive. However desirable, it is in its most literal sense an ambitious aim. It may be necessary to start with the more modest aim—the avoidance of unnecessary and dangerous misunderstanding. If the curtains of secrecy were ever lifted from the archives in all capitals, some of the moments of grave danger in the nuclear age would in all likelihood turn out to have occurred when one side ignored or misinterpreted a signal from the other, or took to be a signal some action not intended as one. Tension can easily be increased if the rhetoric of a speech addressed to a domestic political audience is misunderstood as a deliberate signal of hostility intended for a foreign audience. Understanding 'what is going on in the Kremlin' may be only slightly more difficult for the West than the task of those in the Soviet Union who, faced daily with a mass of information and opinion from the West, often confusing and contradictory, must try to understand, bring into conformity with a certain mode of thought and then predict, the workings of our political systems which are so dissimilar to their own. To misunderstand and misinterpret is all too easy in a world of leaks, denials and off-the-record briefings. The avoidance of these misunderstandings and the prompt detection and correction of them when they occur is an important step towards the lowering of tension. Elimination of unnecessary disagreement would clear the ground for the central task of reconciling, or at least successfully managing, the divergence of interests of the two systems. Even if the once popular theory predicting the eventual 'convergence' of the two systems has few adherents today it is possible to see, in the period we are considering, a growing convergence of the interests of East and West in various areas.

1988 marks the twenty-fifth anniversary of the Partial Test Ban Treaty of 1963, the first agreement signed in the postwar period in the arms control field. This was the agreement which halted the increase in fall-out from nuclear weapons tests; it is a reminder that convergence of interests can produce a valuable and durable treaty. The same year will also mark the fortieth anniversary of the Berlin blockade and will be a reminder that the attempt over the four subsequent decades to improve the East-West relationship and achieve some agreed measures of arms control has not been wholly without result.

Implementing the vision of Shalom in human affairs means working for an increase of trust. Sometimes mistrust is quite proper. Where, for example, there is a real conflict of interest or an adversary is bent on eliminating opponents, mistrust is not only appropriate but essential. It is not the duty of the Church to encourage naive trust where it is not justified. But the trust built up by confidence-building measures is of a different order. The measures may not always be dramatic but it is on such small carefully built foundations that a larger enduring trust can be built. Such confidence building is an essential part of the work of Christian reconciliation.

Summary

One of the crucial themes of this report is that conflict is not to be thought of as necessarily evil and destructive. It is possible to live at peace in a world of diverse and conflicting ideologies and political systems. Conflict does not have to manifest itself alone through military threats. In the midst of our present history we can give substance to the Christian hope which we considered in Chapter 2.

The practical task of managing relationships between the superpowers in East and West is at the heart of this process. If that is to be comprehensive it must include procedures for managing disagreements and moments of serious misunderstandings. The painstaking work of diplomacy over the past 40 years has achieved a great deal and helped in the development of the necessary skills in managing these relationships. It may also have laid the foundation for the East and West to move away from a predominantly military confrontation to a more healthy pursuit of the conflicts between them in other spheres of social and political experience. In establishing a deeper Pax we may be witnessing to the fuller vision of Shalom.

Footnotes

1 *Communications Strategies—An Analysis of International Signalling Patterns.* The Council for Arms Control. Discussion Paper, 1983.

11
The Role of the Churches

Introduction

This report has been concerned to express, analyse and illuminate the many different facets and perspectives of the issues involved in peacemaking in a nuclear age. This has been carried out within the context of a Christian understanding. This final chapter explores the function and role of the Churches in these matters.

In 1982, *The Church and the Bomb* touched very briefly on this issue:

> What role should the Churches play in all this? Should it confine itself to uttering general guidelines which leave room for interpretation so that technologists and others can bring their specialities to bear within them? Or should it go further than this and engage in the technicalities *per se* by advocating detailed and specific proposals? Whenever these and similar Christian bodies engage themselves in detailed and controversial worldly issues, the cry is usually raised that they are not minding their own spiritual business and that they should return to that forthwith.[1]

That Report concludes that Christians ought to:

> relate the Churches' general teaching on war and peace to the circumstances of the present and have the faith to come to specific conclusions, however provisional and imperfect they may seem to be.

Given the precise and directive remit of the 1979 terms of reference for that Working Party, that brief acknowledgement of the issue and decided response was as it should have been.

Paul Ramsey in his work *Who Speaks for the Church?*[2] offered his answer to the perceived either/or choice between on the one hand qualitative and widely accepted generalities about war and peace, justice and sin, and on the other hand specific politicised policy recommendations;

> The purpose of the address of the Church to the world . . . ought to be the broadening and deepening of public debate on urgent issues; it ought not to be to stop or narrow down this debate or polarise the debate that is going on by a finding in favour of a specific policy behind which we are seeking merely to mobilise opinion.

The practice of international affairs is concerned with political judgements and choices. The biblical tradition, in not allowing the separation of morality and public policy, faith and theology, compellingly establishes foundations for political choice. Christian witness is therefore more than individual moral rectitude. It requires a forthright proclamation of religious values and their relevance to the political, social and economic conditions that shape our lives. That, however, is just the beginning of the task. The Church makes many resolutions and preaches the need for peace and goodwill. Resounding resolutions are good but not good enough: the problem remains how to make effective what is known and believed through a process of continuing theological reflection. Here we come up against some basic questions. How much and to what degree does religious faith mandate choice of strategy and tactics? How does the Church find the right balance between describing or prescribing, indicating or specifying? Having confessed one's faith is one compelled to campaign?

This report represents one approach. That is a right and proper exercise of the responsibility of the Church of England in its commission of a study on 'Peacemaking in a Nuclear Age'. The conclusions are now offered back to the Church for debate. The process of the Working Party's work is instructive in itself. A group of people came together to study the issues, to examine both ethical and political dimensions. The dilemma of the extent to which the Church would prescribe on national and international policy was matched by the dilemma of the extent to which the Church should prescribe to its own constituency. The tacit understanding here is that the findings of this report are offered to help churchpeople think their way through the serious issues. Acknowledging that function of the Working Party vis-à-vis the Church gives some insight into the relationship between theology and political choices: the central body asked for a specific piece of analysis from a particular perspective and results of that work will now be used to inform the further thinking. But this is too neat a distinction. Whenever a Church speaks to its own constituency it is inevitably overheard by society at large. The media, for example, publish the findings of reports such as this. Church reports on other social and political issues have immediately been repudiated on secular grounds by governments.

Further than this, the process of construction of this report was itself a microcosm of the Church's role. The discussions on the substance of each section, the different views of different members emphasising different points in different ways constantly illustrated the complexity of producing an agreed interpretation of events within a common theology. The interaction and interdependence of theology and practice and the building of this text proved to be hard and difficult work. The difficulty lies in the importance of accepting the individual perspectives as valid ingredients in the building of an overall understanding. In listening to each other, being willing to offer our contributions as lumps of clay for sculpting rather than unyielding bricks for a geometric architecture emphasised that theology informed and guided not only *what* we did but *how* we did it.

What is meant by 'the Church'? It is particularly important to know how we are using 'Church' in this report. 'The Church' can describe the administrative and bureaucratic structures; the ordained ministry; the full active membership; or all the baptised. The different functions and responsibilities of the Church in each of these aspects leads to distinctive roles at each level of Church life. So the role of the Churches could be that of making resolutions at its Synods and Governing Assemblies. But, as said earlier, these are not enough. A resolution is a statement of the formal position for the Church, but that needs to lead on to the responsibility of the whole Church to use these resolutions as a basis for action. The elected body may have the responsibility of producing the text; the entire body must then use the text as a guide to its own thinking and exploration. So inasmuch as responsibility for political choices cannot be solely that of national political leaders but demands the involvement and contribution of the nation itself, so too there is a two-way process between the elected bodies of the Church and its full membership in the forming of the canonised texts and the subsequent use of them.

Exploring the role of the Churches is not an abstract exercise; it necessarily takes account of the past and present practice and activities in that these have grown out of the Churches' understanding of their responsibility.

The Past and Present History

A brief but excellent account of the statements and actions of the British Churches, particularly since 1945, can be found on p.241 *et. seq.* of the Church of Scotland's 1986 report *Ethics and Defence.*[3] The early 1980s saw three major Church statements— *The Church and the Bomb* report, the US Catholic Bishops' letter, and the Amsterdam World Council of Churches Hearing published as *Before It's Too Late.*[4] In the subsequent years there has been an intensification of the Churches' interest and involvement in nuclear and defence issues, with statements, reports and studies by Church Leaders, official assemblies, working parties, Church-based peace groups, specialist small groups and individuals, plus a growth in the interdenominational and international work and co-operation. Resources have been devoted to establishing institutes and projects, setting up conferences and supporting individuals. Some activities have been to pursue a theological understanding, others a political and strategic understanding. Some are sharply critical of current Western defence policy, others less so. Some see their work as relevant only to the Church and in no way involved in socio-political life. Others are by nature policy prescriptive and operate as pressure groups. Some actions are informal, others backed by the weight of ecclesiastical and bureaucratic hierarchies, with clergy and lay representatives talking with government officials, NATO military and political planners and officials in Eastern Europe and the Soviet Union.

While the issues and topics have focused on defence matters there has nevertheless been the acknowledgement in this Church work of the interdependence with all peace and justice issues: development, human rights, racial harmony, social welfare, etc., and the consequences of those connections have necessarily influenced the work. In 1986, two official groups were established to carry forward work done before: a Church of England Working Party as represented here and the US Catholic Bishops. The US Bishops are examining whether or not they should withdraw the conditional acceptance of deterrence which formed part of the conclusions of their 1983 Pastoral Letter. In May 1987 The Washington Peace Commission published their Inquiry into *The Nuclear Dilemma: A Christian Search for Understanding*.

The listing of activities and involvements demonstrates the Church's engagement in and felt responsibility for political life. In Britain the substance of the reports and resolutions produced by the Churches articulate a growing convergence on several crucial matters:

(a) the conviction that Christians have a particular contribution to make in the process of reaching decisions which fundamentally affect the course of history.

(b) a continued questioning as to whether the use of nuclear weapons or the threat of their use can be justified morally or theologically.

(c) the conviction that the long-term peace of the world cannot be preserved by the present policy of deterrence, which is not a permanent basis for stable progress and genuine security.

(d) the fear that the continuation of the arms race diverts resources from the more fundamental problems of world poverty and the need for a just international society.

(e) a general opposition to the deployment of new weapon systems where these are seen as escalating and further destabilising a dangerous situation.

(f) the conviction that the search for comprehensive disarmament and common security should be pursued with greater vigour and urgency in both East and West.

As said earlier, these statements and resolutions should be seen as the beginning and not the end of the process. While offering a political critique they are made in full consciousness of the need for continued theological reflection and study which need to accompany and follow them. The Churches are involved in a process of engagement with the moral issues and these statements serve to bring public attention to the work that is going on. Statements and resolutions are to be made with a proper sense of humility. The Church needs to accept its own limitations in understanding and interpretation on both theological and secular issues. It issues statements as a reflection of its current understanding and needs to accept that these may prove to be wrong or incomplete. This critical engagement provides a continuing task for theology. The issues themselves provide a common agenda for the whole Christian community which discovers its immediate responsibility through a struggle with the theological and practical issues.

All of this exposes a further dilemma—and one mirrored in the political process. If a Church statement is to speak to the practical reality there needs to be an expertise, awareness and explanation of contemporary issues. Reflecting an understanding at that level would produce a complex text which the Church as a whole may find difficult to comprehend. Conversely texts which are constructed for a wider audience—an audience of varying expertise and understanding—are necessarily simpler and more generalised. These can be dismissed by the expert community as naive. All public texts are constructed for a variety of audiences and for a variety of reasons—for the Church they act as statements of faith addressed both to their own membership and to the political process. There needs to be clarity and agreement about the function of such statements.

The Church's role is not discharged by such statements. They carry with them a responsibility in the Church to continue engaging in the theological process. If that is to be successful it demands an appreciation of realism of political possibilities. Where there are possibilities for action for the Church there are also limits.

What are the Possibilities and Limits?

Each Church, each denomination, is embedded differently and uniquely in its own nation, culture and history. Each has its own resource and limits which will necessarily create a framework within which that Church could operate. A meeting of international and inter-denominational Church groups in Oxford in April 1987 clearly demonstrated the cultural dependency of each. Nor are the limits one way—restrictions may be self-imposed by the Church; they are also imposed by the expectations of a society of the role of its Churches. Within Britain society seems happy enough for Churches to become involved in and devote resources to such issues as development, drug abuse and AIDS but where the issues are deemed to be socio-political such as inner-city deprivation or defence, the observation, comment and involvement are seen as observation, comment and involvement on the government of the day. At that point many consider the Church has stepped across a boundary. This probably says more about the attitudes to those issues than about the Church's role and, additionally, this whole area of tension and hot debate is, for Britain, culture-dependent. The following appears in a small volume *Etiquette for Everyone*, written in the late 1940s:

> Apart from politics and religion, both of which should never be discussed in general conversation . . .

The attempt at separating the Church from politics is unreal. The engagement of the Church with politics is happening all the time. Christian politicians, civil servants and service personnel seek to practise their theology in their work; Christmas cards are fronted with pictures of war planes and regimental crests; the nuclear war planners in the Pentagon pin Christian festival greetings to their doors; Service Chaplains minister to their Service congregations and the Church prays for and works with those in combat. The White House has prayer breakfasts and East-West Church vigils were held through the Washington summit and the signing of the INF Treaty. Religion is interwoven in politics and each must find a way of speaking to the other. The political community may object to Church statements on the grounds of non-expertise, a lack of knowledge of the intricate processes of political decision making, and a failure to understand the complexities. But it is not for theology to develop expertise to the extent it merges with and adopts a political perspective. It is out of the validation and maintenance of a critical distance between the various perspectives that informed choices can be made. All political processes raise national questions as to the values, purpose and direction of the society. The exploration of those questions, the evaluation of our current position to them, and the different directions in which choices lead is the concern of all people. For Christians, theology has a fundamental role to play in that process.

How then are the British Churches to be 'shapers of opinion as well as commentators on policy'? *(Ethics and Defence).*[5] Ought they to construct and validate a position of critical loyalty? Clearly if they are to be a touchstone of our society's ethical and moral codes then they cannot just be like a passive reference book to be pulled down from the shelf in time of crisis. Ethical and moral codes need constant reassessment so that relevant options emerge from the interplay of the basic principles and the realpolitik of contemporary life. Interpreters and communicators have to play their part if such connections are to be made. The questions remain, however, as to how and in what form those theological commentaries should find their voice.

Churches in Action

The following are offered as examples of particular Church involvements; models of action which, within themselves, consistently examine their own philosophy, activity and responsibility in relation to theology:

(i) The IKV, Dutch Inter-Church Peace Movement, has a long history of involvement and expertise in the issues. It carries a strategy of prescriptive demands through a hierarchy—the Campaign Council. The dilemmas they face are several. Given their belief in the changes which are necessary for a lessening of East-West tension (nuclear disarmament which can begin with the Netherlands) they have to be ready to sacrifice the full support of Church membership if they are to hold to those precise aims.

They wrestle with the tension between a campaigning and confessing Church in that IKV is closely woven into the political fabric of the Netherlands. There are regular moments of choice as to the extent and the way in which they might use that position.

(ii) The British Inter-denominational CCADD (Council on Christian Approaches to Defence and Disarmament) is a very different grouping which sees its purpose and function as being part of the network which keeps the issues on the agenda. With a listed and small membership it acts as a forum for discussion, bringing together government officials, academics, clergy, pacifists and peace workers within a common Church commitment. This creates an environment within which people can explore the issues together without coming to a corporate policy prescriptive view.

(iii) Different again is the Washington Peace Commission, a small group of senior Church people, talking with and interviewing senior political and military officials from the Reagan Administration over a two-year period and producing a report on their findings aimed at stimulating thinking at a parish level. It does produce prescriptive conclusions with regard to honouring treaties, research and deployment of certain weapons systems where they arise from the theologically based analysis. The Peace Commission's view of itself is of a Church as an enquiring and evaluating body which operates through the 'gatekeepers'.

(iv) Christian CND is a campaigning and confessing movement within the larger organisation of CND, distinguished by the belief that there is a distinctive contribution to be made from a Christian perspective. It carries a message and philosophy which, in effect, says 'No': a 'no' directed at much of the current policy from a response to and understanding of the Christian gospel. Supportive of positive policy moves towards disarmament and East–West détente, it is nevertheless a pressure group which believes in keeping the debate in the public eye in as sharp a way as possible.

(v) The US Catholic Commission's Pastoral Letter of 1983 followed an intensive period of study and interviews. The conclusions, including a conditional acceptance of deterrence but sceptical about the morality and rationality of any nuclear usage under any condition, were intended to speak to Catholics throughout the United States, including those in the armed services. The hierarchy had sat together, worked with officials and produced their findings in the full knowledge that these would have direct implications for political and military activities, if those concerned acted in accordance with the theological directive.

(vi) The Pax Christi organisation is concerned particularly about educating for peace, a philosophy which acknowledges the connections between international and national harmony. The positive and conflict-resolving stance towards international issues is, therefore, equally relevant to issues within a nation concerned with racial harmony and community welfare.

Inter-denominationally the British Churches are active. The British Council of Churches Peace Forum was established with representatives from all the British Churches sitting on it to establish a place for discussion and learning. The Scottish Churches Peace Team is composed of those within the different denominations with a remit for some aspect of the peace and justice issue and collaborates with the Church hierarchies on a variety of ventures from peace pilgrimages, visits to the Defence Secretary, letters to the Queen, and educational programmes within the Scottish Churches.

Peace and the International Church

The Sixth Assembly of the World Council of Churches, meeting in Vancouver, took on the task of engaging in a 'conciliar process of mutual commitment to the justice, peace and integrity of creation' as a Christian response to the forces and trends that jeopardise the world. While for Britain issues of peace and security may have a local focus in the nuclear threat, the whole Christian community recognises an interdependent world, a world of relationships and delicate balances and a common international agenda. Community violence, famine, injustice, disease are of immediate concern in other parts of the globe: 'You are afraid of death; we are dying,' said a nun from Nicaragua. The Churches as world confessional bodies, and corporately recognising a total concern for humanity, have a particular role to play in bringing together these various concerns. The links between Churches East and West, North and South, offer opportunities for learning through the informal dialogue and can play a unique part in the process of détente and reconciliation. Whatever is pursued in the framework of East-West relations is, therefore, important in its own right but must be done in a full knowledge of a wider responsibility for global security. In 1989 the Conference of European Churches and the Catholic Church are sponsoring a major gathering on the subject of peace. Representatives from Churches right across Europe will be coming together to consider the meaning of the Gospel in the present context of European life.

This report differs from earlier Church reports in that it deals with the nature of conflict, particularly the East-West conflict, rather than with the morality of the way in which a conflict is conducted, i.e. deterrence and war. Because the Church, in the broadest sense, crosses national boundaries, as well as East-West and the North-South divide, it has its own role to play in peacemaking. Proposals for peacemaking are not simply addressed to governments or to those who can influence policy-making, rather they involve local parishes, individual Christians, etc., who represent part of the fabric of society, who contribute to deep-rooted cultural attitudes.

In several East European countries, as in some Third World countries, the Church may be the only institution that offers a political and cultural space that is relatively independent of the state. It may be very difficult to build contacts without institutional support and yet, in many countries, genuine dialogue is difficult through official channels. Hence the Church has a special role to play in fostering the process of dialogue and indeed supporting the development of autonomous social institutions which could, in the long run, provide a foundation for democracy —a necessary condition for East-West reconciliation and for the resolution of conflicts in the Third World.

Soviet, East European, West European and American Churches meet underneath the official language of diplomacy through twinned congregations, joint theological explorations, exchanges of clergy and conferences. There is a growing determination by Churches to build links across political barriers in order that out of a common faith the Churches become interpreters of their own society to one another. The importance of East-West links is matched by the value of West-West links. The United States is an intensely Christian society with active practising Christians in high policy-making positions. The work of the American Churches informs the work of European counterparts, and the links and exchanges need fostering. Churches which share a common tradition in Europe and in the USA could learn a great deal from each other on these issues. The Church people involved in all these exchanges need, and are acquiring, the sophistication and clarity to hold to basic teachings of the Christian faith in solidarity with one another and then encourage one another in their appropriate task of bearing witness within their own society to the implications of these truths.

Conclusions

The Church is not the political decision-maker and does not bear the immediate responsibility for the consequences of those political decisions. While it is true that the ethical base upon which political life operates is built into the fabric of much of the national society, Church leaders are not political leaders and hence the perspective is different as the previous chapters of this report demonstrate. That difference, and the friction it creates, ought to be seen as a positive factor.

Beyond that the Churches have both a moral responsibility and special opportunity to deepen and broaden the discussion and to rescue the word 'peace' from being used or rejected as a political slogan on one side or another. There is a loss of consensus in national understanding of the purposes and policies of defence. There are strong feelings flowing in the traditional peace movements and a widespread unease amongst many informed and responsible groups within the Church membership and throughout society. This requires a level of discussion in which all must be prepared to listen and learn. Without this what should be a sophisticated and patient exchange can become a public confrontation of slogans and catch-phrases that undermine serious debate. The Churches have an important part to play in creating an informed opinion which can draw upon Christian doctrine and ethics and be both supportive of political efforts for peace and critical of particular policies which do not seem to lead in that direction.

In a situation where many people are anxious and often fatalistic or cynical, the Church has a particular contribution to make concerning the long-term hope for the future. The philosophy of defence must be based on something more than an attempt to survive a process of confrontation and increasing arms procurement stretching into the future. An adequate national defence is a necessary but not sufficient condition for national security and, therefore, the way in which the defence posture is mounted matters. Security, to refer to the Helsinki principle, must be translated into economic and social action and not seen purely as a military or even political concept, and is directly related to a Christian view of the world as an interdependent world. The Christian view will also include a hope for the future dependent upon a theological understanding of history.

Within Britain Churches are increasingly being asked or expected by their membership to become involved in some way in the peace and defence issue. This may be at a denominational, diocesan or congregational level but, as evidenced by the variety of meetings and published statements, it is undoubtedly a present and ever-growing engagement. Because of the width and complexity of the subject many Churches are unsure how best to realise their involvement, whether through congregational education, a sophisticated and intensive short term analysis to produce a report or through a theologically-based and politically involved criticism.

There is no one 'right' model. Each Church or group needs to find the model best suited to its own resources, expertise and tradition. Allowing and preserving this difference in witness itself helps the overall Church to understand its role, a role which will emerge as a consequence of accepting the many different perspectives as valid. Acknowledging the inter-relationship and interdependence of the varied witnesses within the Church and using that process to inform a central understanding has a complementarity in the relationship between the Church and politics. The interdependence and integration coupled with a critical distance consequent upon the particular responsibility of each can be used positively to inform a central understanding and witness in national life.

Summary

The fact that a group as diverse in view and experience as the Working Party responsible for this report can work on the issues and produce a statement of this nature and extent is an encouragement to the Church to continue carrying out its own distinctive role in the task of making peace. This chapter has illustrated the great diversity of level and opportunity available to the Churches and to individual Christians in playing their part. At every level, we need continued wrestling with the heart of our faith in the face of these challenges, more communication across the divisions of East and West between the Churches, congregations, and individual Christians, and an effective programme of education to open the way for many more Christians to articulate their concerns and to learn from others of different experience. By such means the Church can fulfil its mission as salt and light in the midst of the hard and demanding work of making peace in a nuclear age.

Footnotes

[1] *The Church and the Bomb: Nuclear Weapons and the Christian Conscience.* CIO Publishing/Hodder & Stoughton, 1982.

[2] *Who Speaks for the Church?* Paul Ramsey. Edinburgh: St Andrew Press, 1969.

[3] *Ethics and Defence: Power and Responsibility in a Nuclear Age.* Howard Davis (ed). Blackwells, 1986.

[4] *The Church and the Bomb (op. cit.)*
The Challenge of Peace: God's Promise and Our Response. National Conference of Catholic Bishops. Origins, NC Documentary Service. Vol. 13. No. I, 1983.
Before It's Too Late: The Challenge of Nuclear Disarmament. WCC, Geneva, 1983.

[5] *Ethics and Defence (op. cit.)*